THE Unbeatable CEO

CLARK VITULLI

THE *Unbeatable* CEO

NAVIGATING YOUR LEADERSHIP
VOYAGE WITH EASE

Forbes | Books

Published by Forbes Books, Charleston, South Carolina.
An imprint of Advantage Media Group.

Forbes Books is a registered trademark, and the Forbes Books colophon is a trademark of Forbes Media, LLC.

Printed in the United States of America.

10 9 8 7 6 5 4 3 2 1

ISBN: 979-8-88750-062-1 (Hardcover)
ISBN: 979-8-88750-063-8 (eBook)

Library of Congress Control Number: 2024903076

Cover design by Matthew Morse.
Layout design by Ruthie Wood.

This custom publication is intended to provide accurate information and the opinions of the author in regard to the subject matter covered. It is sold with the understanding that the publisher, Forbes Books, is not engaged in rendering legal, financial, or professional services of any kind. If legal advice or other expert assistance is required, the reader is advised to seek the services of a competent professional.

Since 1917, Forbes has remained steadfast in its mission to serve as the defining voice of entrepreneurial capitalism. Forbes Books, launched in 2016 through a partnership with Advantage Media, furthers that aim by helping business and thought leaders bring their stories, passion, and knowledge to the forefront in custom books. Opinions expressed by Forbes Books authors are their own. To be considered for publication, please visit **books.Forbes.com**.

CONTENTS

INTRODUCTION

Your Leadership Voyage

Most likely, you were instructed all your career that business is not personal. Bullshit. This approach is the biggest hoax I have uncovered in my fifty-plus years working in corporate America. For decades in boardrooms and HR meetings across the country, the old adage has been proclaimed, "It's just business; it's not personal," despite the incredibly negative impact it has on leaders and their employees.

As an executive coach, I see the detrimental effects of the impersonal approach to business daily. My clients come to me with all the trappings of success—house, car, family, large salary, vacation home, you name it—yet they are completely miserable. As we unpack their daily lives, I see the all too common threads of extreme isolation, frustration with their businesses, and exhaustion from constantly tackling one fire after another. After a mad dash up the corporate ladder or hitting the seven-figure mark, they look around at the walls they have built and realize it feels more like a prison than a business.

Research reveals that CEOs are depressed at double the general public's rate.[1] Also, 70 percent of CEOs who experience loneliness, which is widely accepted as part of the role, say that it "negatively affects their performance."[2] The idea that we can run a successful business without consideration for the mental, emotional, and physical well-being of leaders and the people they manage is antiquated. And it consistently results in personal and professional stagnation, also known as simply feeling "stuck."

Yet, it does not have to be this way. Imagine a well-functioning, efficient, and profitable business where you, as the CEO, feel empowered, effective, and yet free to enjoy the success you have earned. Sound too good to be true?

With a people-first approach, you can easily make it your reality.

PART 1: UNSTUCK

In Part 1 of our voyages, we will uncover the mindsets and practices that do not take a people-first approach to business and, as a result, have left you feeling stuck and trapped, followed by effective strategies that will motivate your teams and free you from the unnecessary burdens of isolation.

PART 2: SET UP TO SUCCEED

Next, we'll dive into the systemic and foundational changes you must implement to avoid getting stuck again and desire long-term success.

---

1   Alice G. Walton, "Why the Super Successful Get Depressed," Forbes, 2015, https://www.forbes.com/sites/alicegwalton/2015/01/26/ why-the-super-successful-get-depressed/?sh=a4c887738509.

2   Thomas J. Saporito, "It's Time To Acknowledge CEO Loneliness," *Harvard Business Review,* February 15, 2012, https://hbr.org/2012/02/its-time-to-acknowledge-ceo-lo.

From redefining your proper role as the ship's captain to learning to navigate positive and negative changes, we'll unpack the tools and explore how to wield them effectively.

PART 3: CRAFTING YOUR LEGACY

For many CEOs, considering their legacy is often on the back burner until it's too late to do anything about it. When you lead with your legacy in mind, decisions are made from a place of greater purpose. This is something my grandparents, whom you'll get to know well by the end of this book, instilled within me as I grew up around their dinner table. When you lead from that place of greater purpose, as a natural result, you will become a better communicator, a more effective decision-maker, and, overall, a happier person.

Aside from a few other thought leaders who have begun to explore these concepts, most of the lessons on leadership I share in this book are not commonly practiced, let alone taught, when it comes to business. It will require that you open yourself up to a new way of thinking, a new way of existing, and a radically new way of doing business. Let's get to work.

PART ONE
Unstuck

As an executive coach, I see it all the time. "Successful" CEOs with large teams, a company operating in the black, large salaries, and the respect of their peers and the business community they are a part of. Yet many, if not all, of them come to me feeling trapped by the walls of the business they built. Work consumes all of their mental, physical, and emotional energy. They are trapped on a hamster wheel of empty promises that if they can just make it through this next launch, quarter, review, or year, things will be different, but it never is. Sound familiar?

It's time to get unstuck.

CHAPTER ONE

Get Out of Self-Doubt and Get Curious

"WE KEEP MOVING FORWARD, OPENING NEW DOORS, AND DOING NEW THINGS, BECAUSE WE'RE CURIOUS, AND CURIOSITY KEEPS LEADING US DOWN NEW PATHS."

—WALT DISNEY

You are not alone. Whether you read the title of the chapter or the summary online, a book for CEOs and leaders who are feeling stuck and frustrated sounds very specific. But as an executive coach and former C-suite executive with over fifty years of corporate experience, I can say with confidence that you are not the first nor the only CEO feeling stuck or even trapped. I'd wager that for most of your career, you have believed you should always know what to do, what to say, what to tackle next. After years of this constant pressure, you've arrived at a place where you find it paralyzing.

Whether profits are lagging, or you're struggling to build the right team, or perhaps the job you once loved is leaving you feeling trapped, or whatever the case may be, the outcome is the same: you feel stuck. Unable to achieve the goals you previously laid out, you now struggle to discern the next right step. A small voice of doubt has crept in, steadily growing louder ever since.

I've worked with dozens of CEOs who are in your exact position, so trust me when I tell you it's possible to break the stronghold of self-doubt and find your confidence once again. The best part is you don't have to have one single answer or expertise. *In fact, quite the opposite, we're going to begin by learning to embrace and ask questions.*

GET CURIOUS

Nate has been a coaching client of mine for the past five years, and in many ways, he's an executive coach's dream client. His company is on a meteoric trajectory, he consistently shows up to our sessions and implements solutions, and he is incredibly driven with a never say die attitude to his business. But do you know what Nate's true key to success is? Curiosity. Time and time again, no matter what challenges come his way, he faces them with an insatiable curiosity. In similar circumstances where I have seen other CEOs pass the buck, and accept a setback as part of the status quo, Nate rolls up his sleeves, gets curious, and boldly tries something new even if it has never been attempted before.

Most recently, Nate was struggling with a massive employee retention problem. While Nate may have been able to take his business from launch to making over $100 million in five years, he was not immune from the perils of the great resignation, which many companies faced in the wake of the coronavirus pandemic. No-shows had become an almost crippling problem among his workforce.

With a sixty-thousand-square-foot warehouse that requires a robust crew seven days a week, as you can imagine, a consistent and reliable workforce is critical. The lost revenue from employee no-shows and the constant need to rehire were taking a toll on his business, not to mention the leadership team's time and resources as they were constantly being diverted away from their roles in order to conduct interviews and train new hires.

Initially, the company implemented a "No-show, No-rehire" policy. If an employee was considered a "no-show," which means they did not call in sick or pre-request time off, they were immediately terminated and ineligible for rehire for twelve months. Unfortunately, the new policy did nothing to stem the number of no-shows, and with the immediate termination in place their workforce numbers quickly began to dwindle.

Clearly, simply punishing "no-shows" was not an effective solution. Nate and his leadership team decided to get curious.

For starters, they began speaking with shift managers and reliable employees, asking for their thoughts and feedback on why there were so many no-shows. Instead of assuming they understood why, they began to ask questions of the people who worked side by side with their no-show colleagues and had a better insight into their motivation. With each conversation, a picture began to form of what their workforce was facing.

Nate's large office and warehouse is located about an hour outside of a major city, in a very rural town. Like many rural farm towns in the South, aside from fast food or retail, there is little in the way of economic opportunity. Nate's warehouse was one of the few additional opportunities available in the small town. Eventually, Nate came to uncover that the inherent poverty of the area was causing a chain reaction in the lives of his employees, making it difficult for them to make their shifts. While raising everyone's wages was not feasible, Nate's curiosity allowed him to develop several innovative ideas that would incentivize his employees to come to work as well as empower them to break the chains of poverty in their lives.

To begin, while his employees' wages were on par with industry standards, Nate set out to ensure his employees could stretch their dollars as far as possible and opened up an "employee-only" general store. The store is stocked with household staples that pass through the warehouse, such as paper towels, toilet paper, and more. Every single employee is able to purchase these items at the wholesale price that the company pays for them, which is far below the retail price they would have to pay at the local big-box store. This is a huge time and money saver for his staff, and empowers employees to keep potentially thousands of dollars in their pockets each year.

Next, Nate realized that his warehouse was right in the middle of a rural food desert, an area in which it is difficult to buy affordable or good-quality fresh food. In fact, the only locations available to grab a bite to eat on your lunch or dinner break were fast-food and at least a twenty minute drive from the warehouse. To combat the long round-trip commute, which was expensive in time and car fuel, Nate hired a full-time chef and opened a restaurant on-site. Employees can purchase meals, at cost, that are healthy, incredibly appetizing, and absolutely delicious, making it a no-brainer for staff members to stay on-site during their lunch breaks, as well as ensure a decent meal when they have a shift.

Lastly, Nate gathered that a significant number of the no-shows could be traced back due to unreliable transportation. Much of the crew were driving cars that were fitter for the junkyard than for their daily commute. Paired with low financial resources for needed repairs and costly gas money, transportation was an obstacle both for those who owned vehicles and for those who were bumming rides. Instead of saying, "That's not my problem," Nate charged his team with finding a way to make reliable transportation accessible to his employees.

They opened up a car lot and mechanic shop. His company now buys older vehicles, repairs them if needed, and sells them to employees at cost. If an employee is experiencing car trouble, they can now simply drop it off at the company-owned mechanic and have their vehicle repaired for a very minimal cost.

Between the general store, the restaurant, and the mechanic shop, Nate is addressing the root issues that are preventing his employees from showing up for their shifts, by not only providing amazing services that would benefit their personal lives but also empowering them to save thousands of dollars every year. Since implementing these programs, employee turnover has dropped by 50 percent and Nate has saved over $100,000 in the cost of turnover. His business continues to achieve record growth and profits.

Mahatma Gandhi once said, "Power is of two kinds. One is obtained by the fear of punishment, and the other by acts of love. Power based on love is a thousand times more effective and permanent than the one derived from fear of punishment."

CEOs are inherently in a position of power over their employees. While, yes, they are performing a service, they are dependent on you for a paycheck, benefits, and more. And since they most likely are not contractors, most employees do not constantly have other employment options waiting on the back burner. This leaves your employees, especially those who are economically disadvantaged, vulnerable. While Nate was fully in his rights as a CEO to fire anyone who did not show up for their shifts and call it a day, he chose to get curious and explore the ways he could positively impact his employees and, therefore, internally motivate them to come to work.

Many times, when facing an issue, we want to use our power to force the behavior that we want from the people we manage. But that is short term, and what I like to call a cheap answer, it's low quality, and will never produce the long-term results you are looking for.

While the "no-show" policy is still in place, using this power to simply punish people who did not show up for their shifts was not solving a damn thing. So, Nate flipped the script and used his power to solve the root problems that were causing his employees to miss their shifts and/or quit. As a bonus, they no longer have to spend energy and resources recruiting new employees. Team members love the benefits and the supportive work environment so much that they are now recruiting their friends and family to come work for Nate too!

> When you lead with curiosity, rather than trying to control an outcome, the solution may not be simple, but it will lead to a long-term quality solution.

When you lead with curiosity, rather than trying to control an outcome, the solution may not be simple, but it will lead to a long-term quality solution.

START ASKING QUESTIONS

Leading with curiosity is typically my knee-jerk reaction, which is in large part thanks to the wisdom passed down to me from my family. Growing up as a Vitulli, business and family were braided together as one. My grandparents, on both sides, immigrated from Italy in the

1920s, started businesses of their own, and then their children, once grown, followed suit.

My childhood consisted of hundreds, if not thousands, of family dinners at my grandmother's house. The adults would be seated around the table for hours after the meal was over. The conversation effortlessly flowed between family matters and business matters.

"Will you open a second location?"

"Have you thought about changing the schedule?"

"What's the plan for the staff this Christmas?"

Over the years, I had a front-row seat as I watched my grandparents, aunts, uncles, and cousins grow their businesses. Night after night, while sitting at the dinner table, I observed as they asked each other question after question, troubleshooting and swapping stories.

Sitting around my grandmother's dinner table, starting at just ten years old I began learning the life-changing power of getting curious and approaching any challenge by first asking questions.

All of our lives, the importance of having the right answer is imparted to us. In school, we memorize our multiplication tables and commit historical dates to memory. Then we go to work for a company, and are told to "fake it till you make it." *And while all of those things are important, when you build a career or a business based on having the right answer all the time, you set yourself up to, at least, get stuck and, at worst, fail.* No one can have all the answers, but anyone can learn to ask a great question that will spark your desired answer.

When you're feeling stuck in your business or in your career, the most powerful skill you can master is the art of asking a great question.

> **No one can have all the answers, but anyone can learn to ask a great question that will spark your desired answer.**

I was very lucky to have grown up in a family that valued questions more than it valued answers. Every Sunday, my grandfather would walk into the living room, a cup of coffee in hand, sit in his favorite armchair, and promptly at 9:58 a.m., turn on NBC to watch *Meet the Press*.

"Clarky boy!" I'd hear him shout as I ate my breakfast in the kitchen, "Come here, have a seat."

"Watch this," he'd instruct, motioning at the TV with a cup of coffee in hand, while I took a seat on the floor beside him.

"Why, Grandpa?" I questioned.

"Just watch," he would answer with a wave of his hand.

And then, for thirty minutes every Sunday, I would watch *Meet the Press* with my grandpa. For my ten-year-old brain, it literally felt like time was standing still as I attempted to watch what I believed was the most boring show ever.

After the program, my grandfather would ask me what I thought about this interview, that story, or some current event. Most of the time, I'd shrug my shoulders and reply, "I don't know," but occasionally, I would have an opinion or question. Each time I did, my grandfather would react as if I had submitted a Pulitzer Prize—winning article, encouraging me to think critically, ask deep questions, and get curious about what was happening around me. *Those stories and our conversations stayed with me for years, but more so was the importance of having a question over having an answer.*

You've probably come to realize at this point in your career that you will not always have the right answer or any answer at all. The good news is you don't have to. Having the right answer will only get you so far, eventually, you will get stuck. But if you can learn to ask questions and be open to new ways of thinking you'll never end up feeling stuck again.

WHAT MAKES A GREAT QUESTION?

While my career has had many chapters, currently I am living out one of my favorites: I am an executive coach to other entrepreneurs and CEOs who are walking the same path I once was. Every month I meet with my four different leadership teams in their individual groups. This allows my clients to connect with peers who are facing similar challenges and opportunities and build a support system.

With every meeting, no matter the group, I begin exactly the same: we go around the room and everyone shares what is working and what is not working, in both their personal and professional lives.

Everyone chimes in with questions when someone shares something that is not working. As they each represent a different industry and background, the questions in and of themselves prompt a robust conversation, often sparking a new idea or passing on a tested and proven solution.

While many of my clients have been with me for years, it never ceases to amaze me the look of frustration that crosses their faces as they share what is not working. Usually, by the time they admit something is not working, they have been trapped in a cycle of trial and error that leaves them feeling as if they are a failure and completely stuck.

> Beginning with a simple question can reveal the answer that was waiting there all along.

That is where the magic of the peer group comes in. Their questions are typically simple ones, but, if executive coaching for over a decade has taught me anything it's that beginning with a simple question can reveal the answer that was waiting there all along.

For our friend Nate, being brave enough to ask a simple question was a game changer. By taking a step back and asking, "What is preventing my employees from making their shifts?" the solution finally had room to present itself.

Throughout my career at Chrysler, and Mazda, and even in launching my own business, I can look back and easily say I never had all the answers. But in every season of my career, I eventually succeeded, not because I always knew what to do but because I knew, thanks to my family, to ask questions first. *You'll never get to work finding a solution if you think you already know the answers. "Answers" will often let you down, but questions never will.*

GET BACK IN THE MIX

One of the biggest mistakes I see CEOs make as they are promoted or their businesses grow is falling into isolation. Instead of surrounding themselves with a group of people with whom they can have honest conversations, they circle the wagons, fearful they will be misunderstood, undermined, or found out as an imposter.

> Organizations where "yes men" surround the leader do not last.

Despite how terrifying it can feel, open discussions, questioning, and thoughtfulness are essential when you're feeling stuck. Looking to scale? Start with conversations. Need to reduce your turnover? Start having conversations. Is a department underperforming? You guessed it... start talking!

Providing a space for open conversations, which I like to call "roundtable discussions," where people can ask questions and share openly without fear of retribution, is key to uncovering the next right steps. When you surround yourself with "yes men," you'll never have a straight answer, and you set yourself on a path to eventual ruin. Organizations where "yes men" surround the leader do not last.

But only asking questions in a room of one is not a conversation; it's an echo chamber, which compounds feelings of isolation and stagnation.

There are three levels of roundtable discussions I recommend every CEO should have on a consistent basis. First with peers and mentors, second with your direct reports, and third, skip-level meetings with people two to three levels removed from you.

1. *Peers or mentors outside your organization*

Not only do these people understand the pressures you face and the nuances of leadership, but they will also have objectivity, which is crucial.

2. *Direct reports*

Your direct reports are your first line of communication, your pulse to what is happening in the organization, and your ambassadors to everyone else. They must access you to ensure they have a clear sense of your vision and can report accurately on what is going well versus what needs improvement.

3. *Skip-level meetings*

Want to know what is really going on in your organization? You need to talk with the boots on the ground. Your team members and employees are figuratively and literally getting their hands dirty. They can tell you, without blinking, exactly how well your systems are working, how happy their fellow employees are, and more.

Roundtable discussions with people at each level will bring clarity and spark new and innovative ideas.

A great example of the importance of these roundtable conversations is my client, Ross. Ross is the CEO of a successful tech company he purchased from his parents a few years ago. While he may have grown up in the business, it's important to note that this early forties CEO was not simply handed the keys to the kingdom, oh no. Throughout his career, he has worked his way up from the bottom. Having held just about every position in the company, he understands deeply how each department and process functions.

Within two years of taking over the company, it had grown from making $20 million in revenues annually to $100 million. Clearly, Ross was doing something right.

So, what's the problem? Ross was absolutely miserable. From being stressed with the day-to-day to absolutely bored from dealing with the minutia, Ross was learning a lesson many a millionaire has learned before him: Just because you are successful does not mean you are happy.

When Ross revealed how stressed and overwhelmed he was, I began by asking a very simple question, "Ross, when was the last time you took some time off?"

Ross's eyes widened to the size of dinner plates, and I could see the calendar in his mind flip back through the pages. Finally he revealed that it had been ten years since he had a proper vacation. This sparked for me another simple but profound question, "Don't you think it's time you give yourself a break?" After taking time to consider his options and connect with his leadership team, Ross decided to take a one-month sabbatical.

No one, let alone the CEO of the company, should be expected to go years without taking some well-deserved time off. Yet for many leaders if someone were to say, "you should take a break," they often shrug it off. There is always too much to do and we think we'll come back around to it later. But when we're faced with a question, it's easier to state a fact rather than try to communicate what we need.

For both Ross and Nate, being open to roundtable discussions made it possible to uncover the solutions to their problems. By answering a question and admitting out loud that it had been ten tears since he had been given a proper break, Ross was able to give himself the permission he needed to take a little time off. For Nate, listening intently to the people three to four levels removed from him gave him the ideas that would ultimately remove their barriers to making it work.

Both Ross and Nate felt incredibly stuck. By getting back in the mix, connecting with people, and being open to roundtable style discussions the solution was able to come to them.

So get back in the mix, have the roundtable conversations, and start asking questions. You'll be shocked and maybe even pleasantly surprised by what you learn and where you have the power to create change.

THERE IS NO PLAN B

There is an old legend about Vikings that I find fascinating. It's rumored that when the Norsemen would land on the beaches of an unconquered land, they would soon after burn the long boats that brought them across the sea.

Why? What was the point?

To solidify in each of their minds that there was no turning back, their options were victory or perish.

When I'm coaching CEOs or entrepreneurs, one of the greatest predictors of whether or not they will be successful is if they are strategizing a "plan B." As we go through their plans for the future, a huge red flag usually sounds something like this, "Well, if this doesn't work, I'm just going to go back to work for my old company. I'm sure they'll take me back."

Or "I'm thinking about starting this second business as a backup in case this plan falls through."

While I'm all for diversifying your income, what is happening here is self-doubt manifesting itself in the form of creating a "plan B" as a safety net. What these CEOs and entrepreneurs don't realize is that by constantly strategizing a backup plan, they're not focusing their energy on their current success and growth.

Listen, I'm the first to admit that life will throw you curveballs, and there are no guarantees that every plan will go off without a hitch. (We'll talk more about that in a later chapter.) But I am here to remind you that fortune favors the bold, so "burn your boats" and toss aside your plan B.

Set your intentions for succeeding and get to work on victory.

Questions from the Vault

Here are a few questions to start with at your next roundtable discussion with your peers or mentors.

1. What did you wish you had known or done differently when you faced a similar challenge?

2. What do you think is the greatest challenge I will face at this next stage in my career?

3. Do you see any unique opportunities that I am overlooking?

C H A P T E R   T W O
Think Bigger

"BIG THINKERS OFTEN DO BIG THINGS. SMALL THINKERS, NEVER DO BIG THINGS."

—KAREN BLUMENTHAL, STEVE JOBS: THE MAN WHO THOUGHT DIFFERENT

When we start out in life, thinking big is easy. We dream of becoming astronauts, prima ballerinas, or award-winning scientists. The sky is the limit. Many CEOs retain this ability, and it's often a catalyst for launching their business or careers.

Yet, as companies, profit margins, and influence grow, so does our fear of what we could lose. Fear is poison, and the biggest side effect it has on CEOs is the loss of the ability to think and dream big. This fear is partially the reason you're feeling stuck. It makes you afraid to trust direct reports, wary of taking risks, and leaves you feeling trapped within the four walls you worked so hard to build. Unfortunately, once you're stuck, the solution isn't as simple as "stop being afraid," but life sure would be easier if it were.

When you're feeling stuck, you've got to start thinking bigger. Begin imagining your business and your life beyond the problems and the fear of "what if?" Easier said than done, right? Well, my friend, the key to thinking bigger is to start listening to new ideas, thoughts, processes, and questions from everyone around you.

As I've shared before, leadership is a lonely business. The more important our title or successful our company is, the more isolated we become. We're left to figure things out on our own, and the pressure to have all the answers all the time is stifling. Listening to the voices of wisdom, experience, and support will empower you to shake loose fear and begin thinking big again. While I hope you take to heart the importance of roundtable discussions, there are a few shifts you will need to make in your mindset if you're going to be able to receive what people have to say and begin thinking bigger. Nothing will change if nothing changes, so get curious and be open to new ideas.

"STAY STUPID"

I walked into the familiar boardroom at Chrysler and sat in one of the fourteen plush leather chairs staged around the hand-carved mahogany table. Over the past few years, I had become very familiar with the space and view of the Detroit skyline from the twenty-second floor. I unpacked my briefcase with a few notes and a pen as I looked around to see the other department heads casually chatting before our quarterly check-in meeting with CEO Lee Iacocca.

"So, how's everyone doing?" Mr. Iacocca asked as he commanded the room's attention and launched the meeting. "We've got a lot of stuff going on right now. What's working and what's not? And don't forget personally as well as professionally."

Sales, marketing, R&D, and more, one by one, each department head outlined the challenges, opportunities, and triumphs their department was facing. The atmosphere was electrifying as we brainstormed and troubleshot new processes and ideas.

It was finally Fred's turn, the head of manufacturing. "Manufacturing is actually doing great!" he declared as he leaned back into his chair with a satisfied look on his face. He crossed his arms matter-of-factly as he continued, "Quality is fantastic, and our processes are rolling without a hitch. Actually…," he stopped short as Mr. Iacocca sharply lifted his hand to silence him.

"Hey hey hey!" Mr. Iacocca interjected. "Easy now. I'm getting reports that our quality is not good."

Fred's arms dropped from their cozily crossed position as he slowly sat up in stunned silence. His poker face attempted to hide the anxiety rising behind his eyes as Mr. Iacocca laid out several reports and correspondences from his COO indicating that manufacturing was in trouble. At the end of which, he looked at Fred kindly and encouraged him in a strong but instructional voice, "Stay stupid."

I have come to understand since that day on the twenty-second floor that Fred had fallen into a trap that many leaders succumb to: the belief that he knows everything. Fred was fully aware of every issue, complaint, and inefficiency Mr. Iacocca laid out for him, but he was dumb enough to think he could handle them independently. Instead of taking advantage of the phenomenal dynamic and collective problem-solving available to him in our quarterly department head meetings, he kept things quiet, thinking he could resolve it before anyone knew.

I would later come to find out that before each of these meetings, Mr. Iacocca would have his COO curate a brief report on each department, so he was fully up to speed and prepared to, if necessary, speak into the dilemmas. What a missed opportunity for Fred on so many levels.

While tragic, it's not unusual for leaders to stop asking questions and assume their approach is right. I see it daily with leaders. When the number of voices speaking to your decisions diminishes, so does your ability to think big.

I truly believe that one of the only reasons why I was so open to Mr. Iacocca's instructions of "Stay stupid" was its similarity to the mantra my family drilled into me: "Be teachable."

Growing up, from elementary school to adulthood, "be teachable" was the advice I would receive from those same loved ones I shared dinner with around my grandmother's tables. The concept of being teachable goes beyond memorizing facts, procedures, and systems and speaks to a willingness to absorb new ways of thinking, opening your mind to ways the world can work versus how you think it *should* work. The core message behind "be teachable" and stay stupid is the same: *never stop learning.*

> If you're going to think bigger, you're going to need bigger ideas, especially ones that challenge your own expertise.

If you're going to think bigger, you're going to need bigger ideas, especially ones that challenge your own expertise. Adopt the mindset of a lifelong learner. Don't assume you're the smartest person in the room; be open to learning, receiving feedback, and being teachable.

LEARN FROM EVERYONE

As CEOs, many of the people we interact with actually work *for* us. In the hierarchy of corporate culture, structurally, you are in a "higher" position. Unfortunately, leaders often make the mistake of thinking their expertise in every area rises with their position, when the truth is you can and should be learning from everyone. From the direct reports to your executive assistant, the team leads you have skip-level meetings with, and beyond, each person in your organization has valuable insight and experience that could revolutionize your approach to a subject.

For example, I have never met an executive assistant who was not an incredible out-of-the-box problem solver and intuitive communicator. Next time you need to have a challenging conversation with a direct report, ask your executive assistant how he or she would approach the conversation and their thoughts on achieving your goals. I guarantee they will have a winning strategy and illuminating insights.

Do you know that intern in the marketing department? Take them out to lunch as soon as possible and ask them for their honest opinions of your company's marketing strategy and processes. They will intuitively understand how to speak to the next generation of prospective clients and customers in a way leadership never will because they *are* that generation. Additionally, they just spent the last semester soaking in the latest and greatest approaches to marketing by their college professors. They will be able to pass that knowledge on to the department if they simply have the chance.

One of the best examples of learning from everyone is the now infamous Duolingo intern, Zaria Parvez. When Parvez first started her entry-level position as a social media coordinator, TikTok was nowhere on her job description or the language learning platform's radar. Thankfully Zaria saw an opportunity, ran point on the direction and execution of content creation for the ballooning platform, and rapidly grew the Duolingo account's followers from forty thousand to four million!

What if her manager had said, "No, Zaria, I don't want you wasting time on content for TikTok. Just post to Instagram and Facebook as normal"? Let's be honest, no one would have faulted that manager as it's a common response to new employees wanting to create a new initiative. But what a missed opportunity for everyone that would have been! Luckily for all involved, that was not the case, and now Duolingo has a winning social strategy and the immense talents of Parvez leading the charge as she has since been promoted to global social media manager.

I can easily reflect on a similar situation from my regional manager days at Chrysler. As I was poring over the numbers for the South Florida/Miami dealers, they all looked pretty grim…except for one. One dealership in Miami's heart was killing it in sales, and, on paper, the answer was not obvious. They had roughly the same amount of sales associates and similar marketing budgets, but this Miami dealership was running laps around the others. I quickly hopped on a plane to see if I could determine the secret ingredient in the sauce, plus a little sunshine and phenomenal Cuban food never hurt anyone.

I didn't tell the dealership owner I was coming in an attempt to get a true idea of the customer experience. Within three minutes of parking on-site, an associate welcomed me to the lot and asked what kind of vehicle I was in the market for. I was immediately guided onto a beautiful sales floor that was pristine and elegantly decorated with soothing colors (clearly, they had worked with a designer) that made me feel at ease and was offered a cool beverage to counter the effects of the Miami sun.

Eventually, I disclosed who I was and was given an in-depth tour of the facility, but the outstanding level of friendliness and excellence I experienced was the same as when I pulled up.

My next stop was one of the struggling dealerships. I was very quickly able to determine why they were struggling. After arriving on-site, it took a good twenty minutes of wandering around the lot, pretending to look at cars, before anyone inquired if I needed assistance. The lobby was dingy and ill-kept, not to mention the disrepair of the bathrooms. The decor was outdated and worn out, and the financing offices looked more like a place to plan your funeral rather than finalize purchasing a beautiful new car. You get the idea.

Finally, I had the opportunity to ask the struggling dealer's owner why he wasn't hitting the same numbers as the thriving dealership on the other side of town. He looked at me passively and said, "Ahhh, ya, he has that killer location, plus he employs way more sales guys than I do." He clearly did not have the "stay stupid" mentality and went on to rattle off a handful of other "reasons" for the sales gap. I finally said, "Gotcha. Actually, hop in my car; let's just go for a drive and take a look."

Within fifteen minutes of exploring his competitor's facility, the struggling dealer had the same revelation I did, and I didn't even have to say a word.

FIND AN OUTSIDE PERSPECTIVE

An outside perspective can be absolutely priceless when you need to think bigger. Whether you're drawing on their unique expertise or the fact that they can offer an objective view, there are several ways you can find an outside perspective that can broaden your understanding of the issues that leave you feeling stuck.

1. Hire outside talent.

While I believe promoting from within is part of a healthy and long-term business strategy, sometimes hiring outside talent can transform an echo chamber into a symphony. Oftentimes it's easy for CEOs to get stuck in the same ways of thinking and difficult to find a new angle. This is where outside talent can be invaluable, especially if you can hire for skill rather than industry experience. The outside talent will bring the best of the methods and strategies they learned from their previous industry, and it's often just what the doctor ordered to inspire outside-the-box solutions and bigger thinking.

2. Get educated on your pain points.

Just because you recognize a pain point does not mean you are educated on it. Reciting your pain points and being educated on them are two very different things. Issues like high turnover, low sales, or stress are easily recognizable as problems. But small thinking assumes you know the cause of the issues and results in Band-Aid solutions. If you have been dealing with the same issues for over ninety days, it's time to dig a little deeper.

Let's use unexpected weight gain as an example. You know your clothes don't fit like they once did, and your energy is low. On the outside, nothing has changed, and your diet and exercise have remained consistent. So what would you do? You research your symptoms, talk to your doctors, and potentially work with a personal trainer or nutritionist. All of this education would give you an understanding of why the weight gain has occurred in the first place and, second, how to get back on track. You have to think bigger than cutting out the alcohol for the weekend or doing a fad diet for a week or two.

The same principles apply to business, but Band-Aid answers are quicker and cheaper. Getting educated on your pain points in your business could mean bringing in an outside consultant like I just mentioned, attending a seminar, or having your direct reports read through a book with you. The goal is to get to the root of the issue.

Say your product development team is consistently behind in the target delivery dates. Do you know why? Perhaps it's because your business development teams are promising clients deadlines before connecting with the development team. So you then bring an outside consultant to conduct interviews with all the team members. Are your developers leaving after only a year? Or perhaps your business developers promise speedy deadlines to keep clients happy and their sales commissions up? There could be several reasons that will require you to think bigger than just the chain of communication if you want to get to the root cause and find a long-term solution.

REMEMBER, SMALL AND STEADY WINS THE RACE

In *Atomic Habits*, James Clear shares, "Every action you take is a vote for the type of person you wish to become. No single instance will transform your beliefs, but as the votes build up, so does the evidence of your new identity."[3]

Learning to receive new ideas and information, thinking bigger, and implementing them will take time. After years of feeling like you must have all the answers on your own, stay open and be patient with

---

3   James Clear, *Atomic Habits: An Easy & Proven Way to Build Good Habits & Break Bad Ones* (New York, New York: Penguin Publishing Group, 2018).

yourself; remember you're playing the long game here, and getting unstuck is just the first step.

Questions from the Vault

1. When was the last time you learned something new or asked an inquisitive question of someone within your organization that you would not normally turn to for guidance?

2. What issue have you been facing for at least six months that would benefit from an outside perspective?

3. What are the plan B's that you need to let go of, and where should you focus that energy instead?

CHAPTER THREE

Reinventing Yourself and Your Products

"SOMETIMES LIFE REQUIRES MORE OF YOU THAN YOU HAVE TO GIVE & DEMANDS YOU PLUNGE INTO THE REINVENTION OF YOURSELF IF YOU TRULY WANNA LIVE."

–CURTIS TYRONE JONES

One of the most effective tools to break out of any ruts or feelings of being stuck is the willingness and agility to reinvent yourself, your products, or your business. Industries, market demands, and people will change. Every marketing expert will share that you will need to reinvent yourself or your product to align with the times if you want to continue to succeed.

The world, and especially our workplaces, is an ever-changing landscape that we will naturally have to evolve with if we plan to survive. I can think of over a dozen people who have reinvented themselves and their careers as industries shifted, passions evolved, and they matured. Take, for instance, Arnold Schwarzenegger, a professional bodybuilder who evolved into an actor and eventually reinvented himself completely to serve as governor of California. Another great example of reinvention is the online retail giant Amazon, which originally started out by selling only one product: books.[4]

Not only does reinvention have a high track record of monetary and influence gains, but it's also shown to be very valuable for our mental and emotional health, challenging us and allowing us to grow, learn, and reach a higher level of satisfaction.

So if reinvention is so great, why don't more people embark on the journey when they find themselves stuck personally or professionally? Well, put very simply, it's terrifying.

> So if reinvention is so great, why don't more people embark on the journey when they find themselves stuck personally or professionally? Well, put very simply, it's terrifying.

When we choose to reinvent, we are forced to acknowledge what we do not know; the hurdles can feel overwhelming, and suddenly, doing things "as usual" suddenly sounds like a much safer option.

But it's important to remember that it's a false sense of security. The Roman poet Virgil said, "Fortune sides with him who dares,"[5] and I do not think he could be more correct. While choosing to reinvent can feel intimidating, consider the alternative, and ask yourself, "Is it

---

4   Dave Paresh and Easter Makeda, "Remember When Amazon Only Sold Books?" *Los Angeles Times,* June 18, 2017, https://www.latimes.com/business/la-fi-amazon-history-20170618-htmlstory.html.

5   Virgil. *The Aeneid,* trans. Robert Fitzgerald and Robert Fagles (New York, New York: Penguin Publishing Group, 2008).

worth it to feel stuck for the rest of my life?" Reinvention can be the difference between long-term success and certain failure.

GET COMFORTABLE WITH BEING UNCOMFORTABLE

I still remember the smell of coffee on my desk when the phone rang.

"Hello?" I answered as I took another sip.

"Mr. Vitulli," the admin on the other side began, "Mr. Iacocca would like to see you downstairs in the studio immediately."

His words caught me off guard. Lee Iacocca was a very measured and thoughtful man who seldom requested something immediately, so I was slightly concerned. "Certainly. Do you know what this is about?" I asked, hoping to gain some sort of insight into what I was walking into.

"No, sir," they responded, "but I do know it's urgent."

"I'm on my way," I said as I slid my coat jacket back on, tightened my tie, and set the phone back in its receiver.

As I turned the corner into the studio, I saw Mr. Iacocca casually chatting with another gentleman, whom I couldn't distinguish from the back of his head.

Mr. Iacocca spotted me and raised his hand out in my direction. "Ah, here he is!" he announced with a welcome tone and a smile. The stranger turned to face me, and I felt the earth shift slightly underneath my feet as it became clear it was the one and only Grammy-winning, Oscar-winning Frank Sinatra.

The crooner turned to me with an easy smile and held out his hand. "It's nice to meet you, Clark," he responded smoothly.

"It's nice to meet you too, Mr. Sinatra," I said while shaking his hand with all the composure I could muster, trying my best not to show my feeling of being starstruck.

"Ahh," he responded with a small wave across his chest, pushing away the formality playfully, "Call me Frank."

"Clark." Mr. Iacocca said my name more like an announcement, and our attention was immediately cast in his direction. "Frank here will be working with us to launch a special edition Imperial. It will be two doors and sport a baby blue color in honor of Mr. Sinatra."

Hearing the car's details, my brain immediately snapped to attention. "What's our timing for the launch?" I responded.

"Forty-five days. Can you help coordinate?"

Forty-five days to market and launch a limited edition vehicle was barely the blink of an eye, but as the head of marketing, I knew Mr. Iacocca's question was more of a mandate. "Yes sir. I'm on it." We were in the middle of reinventing Chrysler, and speed was critical.

It was 1981; we were two years into Iacocca's tenure as CEO and chairman at Chrysler and reinventing what a modern American car company could look like.

When Iacocca came to Chrysler, the prognosis was not good. The big three car companies were facing bankruptcy amid an economic downturn. Also, Chrysler's inventory consisted of large gas guzzlers, and they were losing sales to the smaller, more fuel-efficient Japanese models that had hit American shores.

In addition to finding new sources of credit and negotiating with the unions, Iacocca completely overhauled Chrysler's inventory, swapping out the older low-mileage models for fuel-efficient ones, all the while implementing aggressive marketing campaigns that leveraged the influence of celebrities like his longtime friend, Old

Blue Eyes. Everything about the car industry was being reinvented in those days, but Chrysler more so than others.

From top to bottom, everyone felt uncomfortable with the change that was required if we were going to survive and eventually become profitable as a company. So if the CEO wanted a new product on the market in forty-five days, I would work my ass off to make it happen. When all was said and done, we missed the deadline by a couple of weeks, but its timing ended up working in our favor, and we launched the blue car that spring.

I'll never forget the bold moves Iacocca made in those first couple of years he was at Chrysler. In doing so, he cemented his legacy as a tycoon of industry and a leadership expert.

When we feel stuck, frustrated, or plain failing, our knee-jerk reaction is often to retreat, double down on what is familiar, or try to ride out the storm. What we really need is to think outside of the box, get uncomfortable, and dive in without apologies as we reinvent ourselves, our products, and our businesses.

> When you decide to reinvent a portion of your personal or professional life, I recommend cannonballing into the deep end of change.

When you decide to reinvent a portion of your personal or professional life, I recommend cannonballing into the deep end of change. Sure, it can feel like a shock to your system, but the sooner you make the change, the sooner you can get unstuck and thrive again.

THE LESSONS TRAVEL WITH YOU

In 1998, I found myself diving into the deep end and reinventing my career. I didn't understand it then, but my years of experience working in the corporate car world and then in the recreational vehicle industry were about to converge into one amazing business idea, giving me the confidence and the audacity to launch a brand-new company and be one of the pioneers of a completely different business model.

That year I founded and launched America's Power Sports (APS). Power sports are a subset category of motorsports and include vehicles such as ATVs, snowmobiles, jet skis, and motorcycles. From an entry-level position as a sales coordinator to working my way up the ladder to chief marketing manager at Chrysler and then EVP | COO of Mazda, I was very confident in my ability to make motor company businesses run efficiently and profitably.

Following my time at Chrysler and Mazda, I led several marine and recreational vehicle businesses. I saw firsthand so many small dealerships struggling to make the same transition the big three companies had struggled with in the late 1970s and into the 1980s.

But power sports dealerships are typically little mom-and-pop operations, family-owned and run. Unlike the large corporations, they did not have large banks or the government lining up to offer them the necessary finances and resources. That is where the idea for my business, APS, was born. I could use my twenty years of experience managing dealerships and large corporate car companies and my recent recreational motorsports experience.

At APS, my plan would be to buy up struggling power sports dealerships, optimize their operations, and overhaul their marketing, resulting in a profitable dealership once again, all the while leaving the day-to-day running of the businesses to the families that had founded them.

I did have a few obstacles to consider before launching my business. I didn't have the money on hand to launch such an endeavor, and I had never been an entrepreneur. Both are legitimate reasons that have stopped many people from turning an idea into a kick-ass business. As I paused to think about both of these hurdles, I questioned if I knew enough to launch a new company like APS.

It was at that moment I began to think back on the various promotions I had applied for or received over the years. While I had never done the job before, it never made me less qualified. In fact, it was often a benefit to me as I was not stuck in old ways of thinking. The experience I did have and the lessons I learned, even when seemingly unrelated, traveled with me into my new ventures and were more than applicable in my new roles.

We're often afraid to reinvent ourselves or our products because we believe we are throwing out everything we have done or learned up until that point. Nothing could be further from the truth. Just like Iacocca was able to repurpose the Cordoba as the new Imperial, I was able to repurpose my marketing and leadership skills in a new industry as well as model.

When you're ready to get unstuck, don't be afraid to reinvent and reimagine the possibilities. *The only thing that will hold you back is you.* The hard-won lessons you learned and the expertise you honed will carry over as you reinvent and find a new purpose.

MAKE THE CALL

Once you have decided to reinvent, the sheer volume of decisions that need to be made can be absolutely stifling. There is a reason why many CEOs implement systems, like wearing the same outfit day after day, to avoid decision fatigue. And unfortunately, as a manager, a CEO, and a coach, I have seen how the inability to make a decision can be a silent killer.

Not long ago, I was working with a coaching client, let's call him Felix, who was in a conundrum. He was terrified of making the wrong decision. Like many CEOs in the early days of launching his business, Felix hired mostly family (which should only be done from a place of strategy rather than budgetary, but I digress). For the past ten years, Felix's wife has been the head of HR and finance; she was an extremely talented woman and very adept in the role.

Yet as time passed, Felix and his wife expanded their family with their first child and eventually a second. I'm sure you see where this is going. Felix's wife was in the same position many American women find themselves, working full time for a company and then trying to meet the rigorous demands of raising a family. A study done in 2018 by Welch's found that a mother's work in the home (domestic duties, parenting, etc.) takes an average of ninety-eight hours a week, which is the equivalent of 2.5 jobs.[6] So, as you can imagine, something had to give. Felix's wife began spending less and less time in the office to meet the grueling demands of home life.

Well, what happens next? Of course, a growing company needs a head of HR and finance who is available during working hours. So, when they are not, things begin to fall through the cracks. And when Felix's wife was unavailable to answer their questions or take care of a mishap, do you know who they turned to? You got it. Felix.

As the CEO of a company valued at over $5 million, Felix was constantly being bothered with questions about payroll, staffing, benefits, and more. When he didn't have the time to put out the fires, he would put people off, telling them to return when his wife would

---

6   *The Sun,* "Being a Mom is the Equivalent of 2.5 Full-Time Jobs," *New York Post,* March 17, 2018, https://nypost.com/2018/03/17/being-a-mom-is-the-equivalent-of-2-5-full-time-jobs/.

be in the office. As you can imagine, it made it almost impossible for him to do *his* job, and it wasn't a good situation for anyone involved.

"Felix," I looked at him with a sense of urgency. "I understand that having your wife in the role was a great fit for a season, is that still the case?"

Did I already know the answer to this question? You betcha, but the people you work with will always be more open to a solution if you lead with a question.

"No...," Felix paused pensively before he continued, "I know it's not working right now."

"Have you thought about bringing in someone else to fill that role?"

"Why would I do that?" Felix replied. "My wife is one of the best in the business. There is no way I could afford someone at her level to replace her. Besides, can you imagine how she would feel if I '*fired*' her?" He stopped for a moment and paused, "But I know this doesn't cut it, and I can't continue stepping in to fill her shoes."

Felix was caught between a rock and a hard place. He was too nervous to even broach the subject with his wife, and let's be honest, who else is going to tell the CEO's wife (not to mention the head of HR) that she needs to "pick up the slack" at work? It's just not going to happen. We discussed other potential solutions but ulti-mately I believe he was hoping his team could wait it out until his wife was back in the office full time.

> The only thing worse than making a bad decision is making no decision.

Felix had a decision to make. He needed to either accept that he was choosing to take on the role of HR when his wife was not present or make the investment in a full-time HR employee. Eventually, he connected with his wife, and together they made the tough call to find someone else to fill the role.

The only thing worse than making a bad decision is making no decision. You can recover from failure, learn from your mistakes, set up safeguards, or even innovate a new solution when you make the wrong decision. But by making no decision, there is no chance for anything to change and become better.

As a CEO, I have made hundreds of bad calls during my career, and some of them (actually most of them) were not cheap mistakes. Yet with each failure, I became more efficient, learned what *not* to do, and saw a new way to approach problems. I gained confidence in my problem-solving ability, which is far more valuable than becoming proficient in any particular skill. That experience is valuable and part of why my coaching clients have worked with me for years.

Questions from the Vault

1. What decision have you been avoiding? What is something that you can do this week to move toward making the call?

2. What lessons from your previous work experience could be valuable to you right now? In what ways could you approach a problem differently that you have seen done well in other organizations?

3. Name one area of change that you have been postponing because it would be uncomfortable. How can you dive into the change that needs to be made?

CHAPTER FOUR
Stop Avoiding Your Personal Life

As we walked through the charming narrow streets of Rome, I held hands with my lovely wife, Kim. We had been married for two years at that point and were in Italy for a work trip with Chrysler. The trip itinerary included networking with dealership owners, connecting with my fellow district managers, and shaking hands with manufacturing partners. It was indeed a work trip, but many of the Chrysler employees had the same idea I did and brought their spouses along, each of us planning on mixing work and play. Kim understood it would be a lot of work for me, but finding a few moments to break away would be easy. We planned a couple of special meals away from the group and a Vatican tour we would take one afternoon.

But as the days rolled by, I couldn't find the time to break away. I needed to attend every breakfast, lunch, and dinner, networking like my life depended on it. And while I had the best intentions of taking a morning to explore the Piazza Navona or an afternoon to tour the Colosseum with Kim, I quickly filled up my schedule with one-on-one meetings and attending seminars. Aside from chatting about our day before we both fell asleep, Kim and I had no time to enjoy the city together, let alone each other's company.

As the five-day trip began to wrap, Kim and I learned that most of the couples were extending their European itineraries and tagging on vacation—traveling to other cities or countries and taking advantage of the overseas airfare that Chrysler had covered.

But not us; that was not the case for the Vitullis.

Kim and I would fly home the next day. Between travel and unpacking, I would need the weekend if I wanted to hit the ground running and be back in the office on Monday, ready and waiting to take the calls of any of the people I had just spent the week with and make sure that my bosses at Chrysler understood how committed I was to the company.

Looking back, I see that this trip to Italy was almost a perfect metaphor for my ten-year marriage to Kim. My entire life revolved around Chrysler, and I empowered a dynamic where Kim was forced to do the same.

Day after day, my life was consumed with work; going in early and working late was the norm for me. Over the course of ten years, Kim and I had four cross-country moves. Early in her career, she had worked in accounting. Between my demanding work schedule and raising our boys, we decided she should stay home. In addition to the moves, I was always gone, constantly traveling to visit dealerships or other district managers and the endless list of people who needed my attention.

When I was home, which was rare, do you know what our social lives consisted of? You guessed it, Chrysler. I brought Kim along to company picnics, networking events, holiday parties, and dinner parties. Naturally, her friends became the other Chrysler spouses who were also married to workaholics trying to climb the corporate ladder. What was the point in her making friends with anyone outside of Chrysler when she had no leeway in her life to actually spend time with them?

Day in and out, season after season, this was our life year after year. So, it shouldn't surprise you to hear that eventually Kim and I divorced. I was utterly devastated.

Was I working hard to provide financially so we could create a life together? Yes. But who would want a life like the one Kim was living? No career, no friends, no hobbies, and heck, practically no husband! We couldn't even enjoy a trip to Italy, arguably one of the easiest places to love on the planet. I was trying to balance work and my personal life, but, when weighing the two, work always felt heavier and won out.

What I now understand deeply, that I didn't then, is there is no such thing as work–life separation for CEOs. By trying to keep the two separate, you will only create bigger problems. Your personal and professional life are inseparable, but you can easily learn how to juggle the two.

In our culture, success is defined by the accumulation of money, power, and influence; our families and personal lives deliver none of those. So when the balance scales need to tip in favor of your personal life, it feels counterintuitive. In those moments, we choose career or business, all the while justifying to ourselves that we'll make time later for our family. We put our family and friends on the back burner or avoid our personal lives, thinking we'll always have another chance down the road.

But your family and loved ones are like good health; if you ignore and avoid them, they will go away.

Each time we put our family on the back burner adds a tally to the tab we mentally keep of what we owe them. Eventually, the debt feels insurmountable, or worse; we trick ourselves into thinking that the bacon we bring home makes up for our lack of presence and participation. So we begin to avoid the tab, and our family, altogether.

> But your family and loved ones are like good health; if you ignore and avoid them, they will go away.

You will have to change the way you think about your family if you're ever going to stop avoiding them. Once you do, I guarantee everything in your professional life will flow more smoothly.

YOUR FAMILY IS NOT A LIABILITY

As part of my group coaching program, my clients meet with me privately once a month. This allows a space to prioritize their growth and have those peer-level roundtable conversations. Without fail, at least once in the day, the married CEOs with families will start griping, and it usually sounds a little something like this...

"Well of course John was able to double his revenue last quarter; he doesn't have kids he has to worry about getting to soccer practice and dance recitals."

"Sure, Rebecca was able to visit Japan for a networking trip; she doesn't have a husband who expects her to be home every night."

It's all said with a few laughs and a smile, but the message behind the good-natured joking is clear: *I could be doing so much more if I didn't have this family to deal with.*

While many of these CEOs would never say it out loud or even consciously think of it, the majority of CEOs' words and actions say loudly that they view their family as a liability, often referencing them as if they are another risk they have to assess or pitfall they have to avoid. I was guilty of this in both of my marriages.

It would come out in responses like, "I have to get home in time for dinner tonight or my wife is going to kill me." Or when a boss would encourage me to take some time off, I'd nod and say, "Oh sure, I'll talk to my wife about that. Maybe we'll coordinate something when the boys have spring break." But I knew I wasn't being sincere, and I wasn't going to bring it up with my wife.

Would I have enjoyed some time away from work with my family? Absolutely! But I thought it was more important to show my boss or the board how committed I was to the business.

When you define success as power, money, and influence, your brain becomes hardwired to consistently find ways to deliver more power, money, and influence. We become addicted to the praise, addicted to the promotions, and addicted to the perks of the job that symbolize status. I was good at my job, and I loved the feeling of being needed, valued, and irreplaceable.

The hard truth is, the only place I am truly irreplaceable and where I am completely invaluable is at home and in the lives of the people I love.

Stop speaking and thinking of your family as a liability and flip the script. Instead of "*My wife* wants me home for dinner," change it to "*I* want to get home for dinner with my family." Or "My family will kill me if I cut our trip short for work" to "I am unwilling to lose out on time with my family."

Apply the same ownership, energy, and passion to your family as you do to your business. I guarantee you that when you shift the way you think of your family, you'll find a level of ease that eluded you before.

> The hard truth is, the only place I am truly irreplaceable and where I am completely invaluable is at home and in the lives of the people I love.

People are not dumb; they know that you're way more into your business than your personal life. That is why they go out of their way to make spending time with you easy. They plan vacations they think you'll like, schedule dinner around your commute, and go out to eat at your favorite restaurants, all because they love you and want to be a part of your life. Don't take their understanding for granted. They know you have to work, and yes, they do appreciate all you do for them, but that doesn't give you the license to treat them like a liability instead of the asset that they actually are.

YOUR FAMILY SHOULD BE YOUR FIRST PRIORITY

In my one-on-one meetings with coaching clients, I start every meeting with the exact same question, "How is your family?" In the beginning, my clients often think I'm trying to make small talk, but after working together for a few months, they begin to catch on that it's much deeper. After years of experience, I know that their family should be their number one priority. With each question, I'm retraining their brains to consider their loved ones first, like I should have done in my personal life all along.

People know when they are not a priority to you. So don't think you're fooling anyone when you treat your loved ones like an afterthought.

I know that the clients that glaze over my questions about their family with an "Oh ya, everything is fine" are not engaged with their family, and trouble is on the horizon. Without a doubt, in about six months, their personal lives will be melting down, and they will pause everything at work to put out the wildfire raging at home.

Your personal life, when not tended to well, will always come back to haunt your professional life. Think of the health of your family like the health of your heart. You can ignore your cholesterol, or the high blood pressure. You can continue to push past the warning signs, but eventually one day you will have to pay the piper. And the moment you are having the heart attack, everything stops. Your heart attack is not going to wait for you to finish your presentation. It is officially an emergency that needs medical attention.

The moment you realize your family is in emergency mode, everything stops. It will not matter what launch date you are trying to hit or the contract you signed with a promised delivery date. Your family will need immediate attention and any loving parents or partner will slam on the breaks and get home to their family as soon as possible.

When we think of it in medical terms, in theory that heart attack could have easily been avoided. With attention to diet, exercise, and stress levels, you could have avoided the pain as well as the total meltdown to your personal and professional life. The same applies for your family; if you commit to ensuring you consistently care for your loved ones with time, attention, and affection, you could have avoided your home turning into a raging wildfire that causes everything to grind to a halt.

On the other hand, it's always the CEO who is dialed into his family that is doing well. They are able to tell me about the mental health of their spouse, where their kids are thriving or needing more support, and what the family is collectively excited about for the future. When you ensure your family has everything they need emotionally and mentally, not just financially, you experience peace of mind that will empower you to do your best work.

YOUR FAMILY SHOULD BE YOUR FIRST PRIORITY IN YOUR BUSINESS DECISIONS

As I mentioned, Kim and I moved cross-country four times in ten years. I'm sad to say it, but before each of the moves I never stopped to ask myself, "How would another move affect Kim?"

Your family should be your first priority and first consideration when making business decisions.

- How will adding the new service option affect your ability to participate in your kids' school activities and contribute to the housework?

- If you expand into a new market next year, how will that affect the vacation your partner is planning?

- Is fall really the best time to plan that conference? With the kids going back to school, it's already a time of transition. Will the stress of the conference make it hard for you to support your family?

These are just a few examples of what it looks like to consider your family first when it comes to decisions in your business. Anything that affects you will affect them.

Winston Churchill is credited with saying: "He who fails to plan is planning to fail." And this includes failing to plan how your business will affect the people you love.

YOUR FAMILY SHOULD BE YOUR FIRST PRIORITY WHEN IT COMES TO YOUR TIME

In Gary Keller's book *The One Thing*, he perfectly summarizes why your family must be your first priority. Work is a rubber ball that bounces back; but family, health, friends, and integrity are made of glass. Drop one, and they'll be irrevocably damaged or shattered.[7]

Many of us grew up in families and cultures with the opposite view, myself included. As you know, I am so thankful for how I grew up, surrounded by a large family, many entrepreneurs, and business owners. The general rule of thumb among my uncles and aunts was to always do whatever needed to be done to ensure your business succeeds; your family will be waiting for you.

I took that advice to heart, and you and I both know how that worked out. I see now that it was a different time and different cir-

---

7   Gary Keller and Jay Papasan, *The ONE Thing* (Austin, Texas: Bard Press, 2013).

cumstances. My uncles were small business owners, and I was an executive at a billion-dollar company. My aunts and cousins had each other and a strong community; Kim had no one. Maybe back in the 1950s families were made out of rubber, but in today's day and age, they are more fragile.

In a global economy, where it's now the cultural norm to live hundreds or even thousands of miles away from extended family, the demands of modern life have made families less resilient. Many of the communal and social safety nets that existed for my aunts and uncles no longer exist or have fallen out of fashion, making it imperative that every member of the family is dialed in, especially you.

Considering that your family is a "glass ball" that can't afford to be dropped, they must be your first priority when it comes to your time. When looking at your calendar family events, activities, and time for them should be marked down *first,* and from there you can layer in work demands. Instead of trying to make your loved ones fit into your work schedule, make your work fit into your family schedule.

Finally, when you're with your family, consider the quality of the time you are giving them. You shouldn't be a fly on the wall observing or a simple bystander along for the ride. You should be actively contributing to the conversation, the activity planning, and the overall running of the household.

YOUR FAMILY NEEDS SEPARATION FROM YOUR BUSINESS

Jake, like many of my coaching clients, had a successful business in the start-up phase. Things were going well, but it was still tough. The list of things that needed his attention was never-ending and, as you can imagine, there was never enough time in the day. Five o'clock would roll around, and he would always have the best intentions of packing up and heading home. Most days Jake would text his wife, "I'll text you when I'm out the door in five minutes." Jake's house was only a short fifteen-minute drive down the street, but the problem wasn't the commute.

Lo and behold, twenty minutes later, after getting caught by an employee with a "quick question" Jake was still not out the door, and instead hopping on a quick follow-up call. He'd update his wife, "Putting out one last fire, then I'll be out the door."

When Jake looked up, he realized another two hours had passed, and this time he had a message from his wife, "Don't rush home, dinner is wrapped, and the kids are in bed. We saved you a plate."

This was the routine most nights of the week. Jake would get pulled into one phone call, meeting, or a quick chat, after another. The home was just fifteen minutes down the road, so surely he could tackle one more thing before getting out the door. But before he knew it, it would be 7:30 at night and he missed everything. For Jake, he needed to literally put more space between his house and his office. The short fifteen-minute commute gave him a false sense of security and ease.

For yourself, you'll need to learn how to smoothly juggle both work and personal life. Your family has a different set of needs. They need separation from your work.

As a solution, Jake and his family moved forty-five minutes away from the office, effectively removing that false sense of security and empowering Jake to implement a hard boundary of being out the door, every day, at 5:00 p.m. On his drive home, he would wrap up any loose strings over the phone and then allow himself to be present with his family the rest of the evening.

What healthy separation looks like for your personal life will be completely unique, but if you need a place to start, begin with the 7-7-7 rule. Every seventh day is set aside strictly for your family. Not golfing with your buddies, tackling projects around the house, or hobbies.

Next, every seven weeks is a weekend set aside for the family. This can be a weekend away at a cabin or just a couple of days at home but everyone is intentional about being present. Finally, every seven months is set aside for a vacation. This can be with just you and your partner, with the kids, or even with extended family. It should be at least three days and preferably take place away from home.

Placing the majority of your time, energy, and attention back on your family is going to be a huge change. It may be a process as you shift your priorities and create separation, but I guarantee you it's well worth it. Remember, your business is the rubber ball that will easily bounce back, but shattered glass is a lot more precarious to put back together.

Questions from the Vault

1. Where does my family think they fit on my list of priorities?

2. Looking at next week, what day will you implement the 7-7-7 rule and devote the whole day to your family?

3. Where can you create more separation for your family from your work?

PART TWO
Set Up to Succeed

In the first part of this book, our focus was to get you unstuck, to break past the plateaus that were leaving your business stagnant and you feeling frustrated. And while each of those lessons is important, the work does not end there. Ever heard the phrase, "nothing changes if nothing changes"? In part 2, we are diving into the lessons and strategies that will prevent you from getting stuck once again while also setting you up for long-term success.

Think of yourself as a car driving on an icy road. In part 1, we were focused on towing you out of that snow bank you plowed into. Unless you make some foundation changes to how you approach your business, chances are pretty high that next winter you're going to get stuck again. It's time to upgrade to snow tires.

CHAPTER FIVE

Own Your Leadership Position

In my fifty plus years of working in an executive office and executive coaching, it never ceases to amaze me how many CEOs do not understand the role a CEO is designed to perform. From confusion with how the role is supposed to function, to the drive to micromanage that plagues most CEOs, this is one of the main reasons I see CEOs get to a place where they are personally and professionally stuck. I'm sure that being a CEO will continue to be part of your plan. If you would like to do so successfully, it's important that we take it back to basics, define the role of a CEO, and address the common pitfalls that will prevent you from owning your leadership position.

THE ROLE OF A CEO

A triangle is considered the strongest of all shapes, which is why pyramids, and similar structures, are the most stable of all builds. It's capable of holding its shape, having a strong base, and providing immense support. The same can be said of a CEO who operates in the three distinct functions the role of a CEO is meant to perform. These roles are vision casting, keeping a pulse on your industry, and managing resources for your management team. When you focus only on these three roles, you become like a pyramid, providing an incredibly stable and supportive structure for your team and organization to build upon.

CASTING VISION AND DIRECTION

The main role of any CEO is to cast the vision while ensuring the company is headed in a profitable direction, followed by communicating to your team that direction so they can manage their departments accordingly.

Think of a company like a ship. The CEO is the captain, charting the course and setting a heading, making sure the boat is going in the right direction, and communicating to your crew where it needs to go. Your job is to keep a weathered eye on the horizon and ensure that you are indeed headed in the right direction. Essentially the CEO should always have their gaze fixed outward, taking in the landscape of what is happening, anticipating any icebergs that their teams may encounter, and strategizing a plan to navigate these obstacles.

Now, many CEOs are often also doing the work of a COO, which, in our boat analogy, the COO is the first mate, who makes sure each area of the ship, from the engine to the navigation system and more, is in good running order. Essentially COOs manage the internal process and CEOs keep an eye on the external. CEOs who really are struggling with their roles are truly in the weeds, acting as the COO or in a worst-case scenario with their hands on the axe cutting down trees.

While many CEOs think they can also do the role of the COO, this is a mistake. If your gaze is focused inward on the internal operations, you're not keeping an eye on the external. CEOs are surprised when they find that their company has veered off course and are shocked when a challenge arises seemingly out of nowhere. The simple truth is that you cannot be in two places at once, and your company will suffer when you try to split your time in half.

> If your gaze is focused inward on the internal operations, you're not keeping an eye on the external.

KEEPING A PULSE ON THE INDUSTRY

In line with looking outward, your next role is to *keep a pulse on your industry* so as to stay up to speed on the latest trends and technologies. Like circumventing an iceberg, if you wait until a trend is directly in front of you before you take advantage, it's too late. And we all know how that turned out for the Titanic.

If your competitors have adopted a new operating system, you should be in the know. Or if the clientele is regularly requesting a particular service or upgrade, you need to have a pulse on it. *These critical factors can affect the direction you decide to take the ship.*

ENSURING LEADERS HAVE WHAT THEY NEED

Once you have your vision and charted the course, it's then up to your COO or department heads to set the goals in each sector of your company. Just like the ship captain shouldn't be calculating how much fuel the engine needs, you should not determine how many ads the marketing team needs to run on socials. With your eye on the horizon, you set goals for the company, and with their gaze fixed internally, your leadership team should determine the internal goals to meet them.

Just as a captain would empower his head engineer to make a fuel purchase, you've got to pass on the authority and the resources for your leadership team to make their department flow smoothly. If your departments consistently say they don't have the manpower or resources to meet their goals, it's up to you to get them what they need.

STOP MICROMANAGING

Now that we have clearly defined what the role of a CEO is, it's imperative that you stop any and all micromanaging. You have to pick between steering the ship, which results in long-term success, and continuing to stick your nose into the daily minutia. Being involved in the day-to-day often results in a quick pat on the back for the CEO, but for the company, it results in death by a thousand cuts.

Taylor is one such CEO whose micromanaging is setting his company on a path to self-destruct. Taylor's growing digital marketing agency is still in the start-up phase, but after only a handful of years, he has a full-time staff of about twenty creatives, acquired a video production company to meet clients' needs, and brought in about $6 million in revenue annually. Despite the overall rapid growth, Taylor's marketing agency was struggling.

> Being involved in the day-to-day often results in a quick pat on the back for the CEO, but for the company, it results in death by a thousand cuts.

Over the course of the past two years, the tenure of the average employee had dropped from three years to eight months. Just when they would have a fresh batch of new team members hired and trained, there would be another round of resignations. While a few of his founding clients were still loyal, new client retention was rapidly declining.

Taylor, his VP of Accounts, and the head of HR struggled to understand the constant turnover. You see, the company offered unlimited PTO, a comprehensive benefits package, including legal insurance, and a flexible remote working policy. Yet, when I began to peel back the layers, a theme emerged. Taylor was deeply embedded in almost every detail of every client's account.

Acting as head of business development, almost all new business was brought in by Taylor. Or if a client was referred, Taylor would conduct sales meetings and begin the onboarding process. From there, he would, in theory, pass the client to an account manager, often with incomplete information on deliverables, timelines, budget, and more, thus driving the account managers to repeatedly reach out for needed information.

Taylor insisted on seeing every deliverable before it was presented to the client, often asking for additional rounds of revisions. This would cause the creative teams to often miss deadlines and then create a backlog of work. Once a deliverable was ready for presentation to the client, Taylor would sit at the meeting. Often taking over the presentation, he would go on to make additional promises to the client and set unrealistic delivery dates without consulting with the account manager.

Additionally, Taylor would often issue a directive to an employee in one meeting, forget, and then give them the opposite directive in a follow-up meeting. So to say Taylor was "lost in the weeds" would be a gross understatement. He was a huge bottleneck of information and a large source of frustration for the teams, unwittingly doubling or tripling their workload. No wonder they were quitting left and right.

Taylor did not understand that while he was the final *decision-maker, he was not the* only *decision-maker.* And unfortunately, his story is not a rare one. For CEOs, the instant gratification that comes from being that decision-maker is often addictive. While captaining a ship is rewarding the wins can often feel few and far between. Getting into the day-to-day details and sitting in on client calls was a quick win, but Taylor's business was unsuccessful. Taylor's refusal to allow the VP of Accounts to lead the account managers, and the account managers to run point with the clients, set off a domino effect that will eventually result in a failing business.

> Being a CEO is not a fifty-yard dash; it's an ultra-marathon.

Maybe you have found yourself coordinating a meeting or stepping into a department's process and insisting you sign off on something that you're technically paying someone else to review. *Stop it!* Whatever it is, you've got to get the day-to-day operations off your plate as fast as possible. This is not college; you're not going to get an A+ from the professor by Friday. Being a CEO is not a fifty-yard dash; it's an ultra-marathon.

Here are some of the common red flags that you are micromanaging:

- You're involved in day-to-day ops.

- You approve every task or stage of a project.

- You often give overcomplicated or intricate instructions.

If you recognize yourself in Taylor's story or some of those red flags, then it's time to wean yourself off of the addiction to quick wins. Remember, you can either cast the vision and direction or be involved in the minutia; it's impossible to do both.

Empower Your Direct Reports to Be the CEO of Their Own Department

Once you've set the intention to step out of the internal operations, you will only stay out if you empower your direct reports to be the CEO of their own departments. Otherwise, you'll find yourself sucked into the day-to-day decision-making. Your COO and other direct reports should be the CEO of their own departments.

Give Them Boundaries but Total Freedom within the Boundaries

From budgets to deadlines or simple operating systems, if your leadership team is operating within some set boundaries, they need to have total freedom to run their department within those boundaries. Release them from unspoken expectations that they need to come in under budget, and resist the urge to insert yourself into their individual projects and join their meetings. No one does their best work when they feel like their boss is constantly looking over their shoulders. This doesn't mean they won't be held accountable if things go sideways, but you'll never free yourself up to have your eye on the horizon if you're managing how your leadership team runs their departments.

Run with Their Recommendations as Opposed to Imposing Your Own

This one is especially difficult for my coaching clients who have worked their way from the ground up in the company. Sure, you've done their exact job before, or maybe your expertise is in their department, but that is not your role anymore. If you need to challenge their method or approach because you've made a mistake you think they will make, do so with questions:

- *"What's your plan if the shipment is delayed?"*

- *"Have you considered what the fallout would be with the client if that team member quits?"*

- *"Did you check with Tom to see if his department can make that goal? What did he say?"*

Get them to consider the results you foresee happening on their own, and they ultimately will become an even more valuable and content employee.

Empower Them to Make Decisions without Your Approval

Just as you are empowered as the CEO to set the vision and direction for the company, your leadership team should be able to make decisions without your approval. Insisting that you sign off on every task or project will only make you the source of bottlenecked decisions and undermines your leadership team's authority among employees and the other people you do business with.

> If the idea of setting some of your team loose to make the call on their own is unsettling to you, you either have control issues or the wrong person in the job.

If the idea of setting some of your team loose to make the call on their own is unsettling to you, you either have control issues or the wrong person in the job. If it's the latter, get to work finding someone you can trust and put them in that position; if it's the former, go to therapy and stop making it your team's problem.

Questions from the Vault

1. Which of the elements of the CEO do you struggle with the most?

• Casting vision and direction

• Keeping a pulse on the industry

• Ensuring your leadership team has what it needs

2. What is one thing you can do in the next ninety days to strengthen your skill?

CHAPTER SIX
Build a Successful Team

To simply say that you cannot do it all on your own is a gross understatement. Building a team will make or break your long-term success. Not only will a great team result in greater efficiency and productivity, but it will empower you to do your best work as well. A phenomenal team is not defined as successful because of their KPIs or even able to get the job done quickly. The hallmark of a successful team is their ability to run the company smoothly when you are not present.

For many people, this approach sounds counterintuitive. When first building your business or making your way up the corporate ladder, you're often operating lean and mean. For entrepreneurs, it's not uncommon to act as the CEO, CMO, head of HR, and accountant all in one day, when first starting your venture. You wear all the hats as best you can, with the dream that one day you'll be able to build out your team.

> **The hallmark of a successful team is their ability to run the company smoothly when you are not present.**

The same can be said of anyone who has made their way from the ground up inside a company. Whether you started out in the mailroom, warehouse, or as an intern, you know each role and department inside and out. You've had the bad boss or the awesome coworker, and you've made the mistakes, found the best systems and know the right person to call when you need the order rushed. With your years of experience and expertise, you're practically a ninja.

The only problem with becoming the expert in every department of your company is the nagging belief that no one can do the job quite like you. I've seen CEOs who are simply unwilling to hire key positions like a CFO or even an HR manager because they think "I can just do it myself." Or newly promoted executives who move like molasses when it comes to finding their replacement. Sure they were a phenomenal CMO, but it's no longer their role, yet they are slow to let anyone take over the position.

The result is a CEO who is stretched way too thin. They are still trying to wear all the hats while captaining the ship, unwilling to hire the team they need or micromanaging the people who are working for them. This results in frustrated employees, and a stretched-thin CEO who barely has enough time to do their own job, let alone have a personal life.

A LinkedIn post by Doug Leeby, the CEO of a software development company based in Florida, perfectly shows how this dynamic plays out.[8]

"Wife: 'Let's do something fun and take several weeks off to celebrate our 30th anniversary.'

Me: 'Sounds good, but we can only take a week. Lots going on at work, and I can't miss that much time.'

Wife: 'I thought you said you hire people smarter than you.'

Me: 'Guess I married smarter, too. Several weeks it is!'

"I'll be taking a break from work and LinkedIn, and the one thing I'm not worried about in my absence is Beeline. So lucky to be surrounded by amazing leaders and colleagues. Thanks, team."

While I'd like to take a moment to applaud Doug for taking his wife's prompting, trusting his team, and taking several weeks to spend with his family, this outcome is the exception and not the rule. Just like Doug was initially unwilling to step away longer than a week, many CEOs are unwilling to step away from their business for a few hours, let alone a few weeks. Their anniversaries, kids' milestones, and life pass them by while they are focused on meeting quarterly goals and rearranging the warehouse for the most effective storage solutions.

When you assemble a highly qualified team of managers, department heads, and executives, whether or not they are qualified to get the job done should never come into question. That is what the vetting process when you're hiring for the position is for. You should fully be able to turn each of them loose to do their job with minimal, if any, interference or assistance from you.

---

8   Doug Leeby, LinkedIn, 2022, accessed December 19, 2022, https://www.linkedin. com/feed/update/urn:li:activity:6964946539999838208/.

Yet many CEOs treat their leadership team as if they are a babysit-ter of their department rather than capable co-parents that they can trust to make the right call, leaving detailed instructions, constantly checking in, and giving them very little leeway to actually run the show, which results in a stressed team that is frustrated by the culture of micromanaging you've created.

Once you implement strategies for building a successful team, you'll have the freedom to do your job of captaining the ship while each of your team members is empowered to do theirs.

GREAT WORK CULTURES FOSTER SUCCESSFUL TEAMS

It was 1990, and I stepped into my new role at Mazda. As part of my duties, I managed two receiving ports, the first in Newport, California, and the second in Jacksonville, Florida. It became clear early on that we had a significant problem in the Jacksonville port. I didn't know it at the time, but the lessons I learned from tackling this problem would become instrumental in my leadership style.

After the cars made the trip from Japan to the United States, upon arriving in port, the car would then be customized. These cus-tomizations included truck bed linings, tow hitch installations, and more, before making the last leg of their journey to the dealerships.

Shortly after I had taken on the role, I began receiving calls left, right, and center from the dealers, complaining of defective and poor-quality work when it came to customizations. Being the proactive go-getter, I set to work compiling a comprehensive report and outlined a corrective action plan to rectify the issue. As someone new to my position, I was eager to prove myself and show my leaders that they had the right man for the job. After four weeks of research, my presentation was buttoned up and ready to roll. I requested an hour of the board's time to share my findings.

The fateful day came, and I gave my presentation with confidence; I just knew I was going to knock their socks off with my impressive plan. As I ran point by point through my presentation, every member of the board, all of them visiting from Japan, listened intently and nodded politely.

When I wrapped my report, the CEO looked at me kindly and said, "Clark, that was excellent."

Yes! I have got this in the bag. I thought to myself.

Then he continued, "It's clear you spent quite a lot of time and effort putting together a truly comprehensive report and correction plan, but we are aware of the issue in the Jacksonville port. We have been preparing and planning a corrective plan for the past six months and will implement it in just a few weeks."

I was flabbergasted. On the one hand, I felt like a heel. A five-minute call to see if they were aware of the issues in the first place would have saved me hours of research and planning, not to mention the hour of the board's time—which I had just wasted.

On the other hand, the CEO and the entire board were so kind, gracious, and appreciative of my efforts. I had never seen anything like it. If this were an American company or an American board, they would have cut me off five minutes into my presentation and sent me home with my tail tucked between my legs. Not these guys; they made me feel as if I was no less valuable.

In my time working with my Japanese counterparts, I would see this again and again. They did everything with absolutely perfect planning and surgical execution, in addition to being warm, kind, and understanding. As a rule, they never operated from a place of needing to "put someone in their place" to get results.

Was I ultimately out of my league, and did I waste an hour of the board's time? Yes. Was I an extraordinarily proactive and go-getter employee who was committed to excellence? Absolutely. My Japanese superiors still valued me as an essential part of their team, which showed. This experience was one of my first glimpses into what it means to truly appreciate the people in your organization.

As you can imagine, my loyalty went through the roof. Their culture of respect, kindness, and graciousness allowed me to continue to do my job with confidence and grow as a professional. It is just one of the reasons why I enjoyed my time at Mazda as much as I did.

At Mazda, I was valued as a person first, and it showed. While you can pay your team well, offer awesome benefits, and have each person working in their preferred role, those benefits in and of themselves will not build loyalty. You will also need to cultivate a great working environment based on trust, respect, and kindness, even when someone seemingly "wastes" your time. That, combined with the other perks I mentioned, created the needed recipe to build loyalty and a team that will partner with you for years to come.

PASS ON YOUR INSTITUTIONAL KNOWLEDGE

As I mentioned earlier, chances are you've worn quite a few hats during your career or tenure at your company. You know the ins and outs of the company like no one else, which leaves you feeling like no one else can do your job. But if your business is going to run smoothly without you, it's critical that you get all that fantastic institutional knowledge out of your head, and into the hands of your leadership team.

While training materials and videos can and should be developed, it's more important initially to get out of the weeds of actually doing the work and instead spend some dedicated time training your team in what you know. Have you ever found yourself saying, "It's just faster if I do it myself"? While true, you probably know by now that it's a slippery slope that just leaves you stuck in the weeds and not captaining the ship.

One of the best things you can do to correct this dynamic is make a large time investment up front, stop losing your day in five minutes here or ten minutes there increments. Over the next ninety days, pick one day for each department head or leadership team member and block out your calendar solely for them. During that time, address any pressing issues they are facing, and make it a priority to pass along any and all institutional knowledge you have about their department or role.

In preparation for your training day, I always suggest keeping a document open on your computer, continuously noting the systems, processes, or information that occur to you that you will need to pass on. This can be anything from a preferred vendor for a specific part to the best system for scheduling warehouse teams and beyond. The key is to get the information out of your head and into the hands of the people who need it. This can also provide a needed opportunity for your team to review with you new and improved processes they would like to implement.

Passing on this institutional knowledge will not only empower your team to be successful in their everyday operations but also set you up for long-term success. You'll free yourself of the day-to-day minutia that weighs you down and prevents you from being a bottleneck of decisions or information. Just imagine a world where you are doing *only* your job, because you trust everyone else to do theirs!

HIRE PEOPLE WHO HAVE THE SKILLS YOU LACK

Determining the right people to add to your team can be daunting. A new hire can make or break your quality of life when it comes to your job. I always recommend, when in doubt, to begin by hiring the people who have the skills you lack. If you can't afford a full-time hire, rent them! From a part-time executive assistant, a fractional CFO, or contracting a marketing company, the key is to bring in support where you need it the most.

When I founded APS, the focus was to work specifically with motorcycle and power sports dealerships, acquiring the struggling dealerships and transforming them into successful businesses. Had I ever owned a motorcycle before? Nope. Heck! I rode on the back of a motorcycle once with my brother, and that was enough to scare me. But I knew how to sell vehicles and knew what dealerships needed to be successful. And after just a handful of years, I grew APS to the second-largest motorcycle/power sports dealer group in the United States, acquiring seventeen dealerships and sixty-three brands with 635 employees in seven states from California to Massachusetts. Yet, I began with much more humble beginnings, working from the living room of my apartment with barely two nickels to rub together. Luckily, I had some amazing financial backers and enough start-up funds to pay myself a salary and hire just one employee.

If you have ever been a solopreneur or needed to build a department from the ground up, then you know that your first hire is critical. Should I hire a tech who could speak the language of the engines and makes/models? Or perhaps my first hire should be a marketing pro familiar with the power sports industry? After all, if I want to turn these dealerships around, sales will be key. There were several gaps that would eventually need to be filled.

I stepped back and took a bird's-eye view at what the next twelve months would require to get the business off the ground. Suddenly I saw an endless stream of meetings, phone calls, paperwork, and spreadsheets as I did the work of identifying the dealerships, negotiating with the owners, and finalizing the purchases. I knew instantly that I would need a kick-ass executive assistant who could run my schedule, who could be entrusted with communication, and who possessed military-grade organizational acumen. All areas that I struggle to stay on top of. I immediately thought of the executive assistant from Chrysler, Rachel. I gave her a call and she accepted a job that day.

Building a successful team is a lot like planning a wedding. The second you say you're getting married, you will have a dozen different vendors who all claim that their service is critical. The florist thinks the flowers will be the most important; the baker does the same for the cake, and so on. Similarly, when you're outfitting your company or department, finance people will tell you it's all about the numbers, creatives will tell you it's all about the branding, marketing will say it's all about ad production, you get the idea.

While every role is important, start by filling in the largest gaps in your own knowledge. Maybe you're like me. My background was in marketing and communication, and you can carry that for a bit, but you struggle with staying on top of the numbers. Hire someone who can manage the budget, keep an eye on cash flow, and help you set purchasing goals. When you can find someone who can fill the gaps, you'll be able to do what you do best and scale quickly.

This same concept can be applied to a team that's in place but maybe consistently struggling to make its objectives. Look at the gaps in the team and evaluate how you can hire someone to fill them. Perhaps there is only one guy in the warehouse with a license to drive the forklift, and when he calls in sick, it causes a huge bottleneck. Get someone else trained, fast! Or maybe your head of public relations is swamped and needs support. Hire a second person or get them an assistant to free up their time. Additionally don't expect team members to all "pitch in" to fill the needs of another full-time position. They already have full-time jobs.

The key is to look at your skills or the skills of your team members, talents, education, and/or natural giftings and determine what is missing. That missing puzzle piece can make all the difference and empower you or your team to operate much more effectively and with ease.

MAKE DECISIONS WITH YOUR HEAD, HEART, AND GUT

When building a team, you have to remember you're leading people, not spreadsheets. While many trains of thought tell us that data always give us the answer, the truth is you're going to have to make decisions from your head, your heart, and your gut. Let's dive into a hypothetical situation to demonstrate where and why it's important to use all three.

Your Head

Let's start by considering that one employee who you have a great personal connection with, but who is consistently underperforming. While you enjoy working with them, they make life difficult for their entire team. Usually, their department has been consistently struggling to meet goals quarter over quarter.

This is a perfect example of when you need to use your head. Yes, you like them, but is the drain they cause on morale and resources sinking the boat? Team members like this often get labeled as teachers' pets, and usually, it's not long before the other employees' resentments build up and spur them to look for a company where their talents will be appreciated.

Now, making a decision with your head does not mean you need to fire them. It could mean working with HR to develop a performance plan or finding them a role they are more suited for. I know your heart is telling you they are amazing, but sometimes you have to consider your bottom line, balance it with team morale, and then make a decision accordingly.

Your Heart

Next, let's take a look at your high performer, the one who hits every KPI on time, if not early, and makes it look easy. But they also happen to be the employee who makes everyone miserable. Perhaps they are short-tempered, rude to their coworkers, or passive-aggressive. Essentially they can be counted on to do two things: first, get the job done, and second, take the energy in the room way down.

With these high performers, it's easy for you to dismiss their poor bedside manner with a cheap answer such as "it's just business. Don't take it personally." After all, the numbers on the spreadsheet will usually convey you'd be crazy to ever let them go. But you've got to make a decision with your heart on this one because your goal is not to have a successful employee but a successful *team*. If one person is making everyone's life a living hell, your team will not be successful.

Your Gut

Finally one of the most important times you can use your gut to make a decision is when you're interviewing candidates for a role. While you may come across someone who has all the experience in the world, if you are not sure they are going to treat your team with kindness, respect, and trust, they won't be a good fit.

> Listen to your gut in these instances; it's very seldom, if ever, wrong.

The reverse is also true in this situation; I can't tell you how many times I made a hire who, on paper, was not considered qualified. A sixth sense takes over and I somehow just know they are perfect for the job. Sometimes it's the way they carried themselves, or something in a referral letter, or how they spoke to my assistant when scheduling. There is something special I can only describe as a gut feeling, and it tells me they will kick ass.

Listen to your gut in these instances; it's very seldom, if ever, wrong.

Learning to make decisions with your head, heart, and gut can be terrifying when most of us live in a world that only sanctions decisions made from our head. Give yourself time to find the balance, to listen to the small voice when something "doesn't feel right," and, above all, remember your goal is to build a successful team.

Questions from the Vault

1. How would my employees or my team describe the working environment?

• If trust, kindness, and respect are not some of the adjectives used, what is one thing you can implement immediately to move the company in that direction?

2. What institutional knowledge have I been holding onto that needs to be passed down?

3. Which of the three decision-making areas (head, heart, and gut) do I struggle to listen to the most?

• What is one thing I can do this week, to tune back into that area?

CHAPTER SEVEN
Evolve with the Times

"CONSCIOUS LEADERSHIP OCCURS WHEN LEADERS PERSISTENTLY REVISIT THE SET VISION TO VERIFY THEIR RELEVANCE AND HOW FAR THEY STILL NEED TO GO FOR THAT VISION TO COME TO PASS."

—GIFT GUGU MONA, THE EFFECTIVE LEADERSHIP PROTOTYPE FOR A MODERN-DAY LEADER

Many of us imagine ourselves as mavericks. We launch into our careers with a deep desire to create change. We're happy to disrupt the system, implement a new approach, or challenge how things have always been done. Until we attain a certain level of success, suddenly all that talk of revolutionizing the place goes out the window. We go from "Let's make things better!" to "Things are pretty good. Why fix something that's not broken?"

Our desire to create change is replaced by a feeling that we need to protect what we perceive is already working for us. It's one of the easiest snowbanks you can plow right into. Without fail, CEOs experience incredible resistance to evolving when it comes to attracting and retaining the next generation of talent.

"It's these damn Millennials...."

I could purchase a small island if I had a dollar for every time I've heard this one, usually as a precursor to how this generation's demands are detrimental to their business. Many CEOs, and even some of my coaching clients, love to dismiss legitimate issues in their company culture and systems by blaming the values of the next generation. What is working for the CEO is no longer working for the next generation, and there lies the tension.

Today it's Millennials taking the brunt of their vitriol and Gen Z not far behind, but during my time at Chrysler, it was the Generation Xers we pointed the finger at, looking down on them for "not getting with the program." Blaming the next generation and their values, or perceived lack thereof, is an easy way to avoid actually addressing the challenges of the day.

Maybe you've heard yourself saying one of the following...

- It's these damn Millennials... they have no sense of loyalty and jump companies as soon as they are offered more money elsewhere.

- It's these damn Millennials... they don't want to work, and leave as soon as the clock strikes 5:00 p.m.

- It's these damn Millennials... they are constantly requesting time off or a pay raise.

Do any of these sound familiar?

With two Millennial sons of my own, whom I've raised and watched enter the workforce, I can testify firsthand that they, and Gen Z, approach work and their careers from a completely fresh perspective. It's true; they don't want to stay late at the office or come in early before the sun comes up. It's also true that the average Millennial and Gen Zer remain at the same job for less than three years.[9] A study conducted by Gallup even revealed, "Millennials are the least engaged generation in the workforce. Only 30 percent are engaged while 55 percent are not engaged, and 15 percent are actively disengaged."[10]

No wonder they are an easy scapegoat when it comes to finding someone to blame your problems on.

Don't get me wrong, I think your frustrations are legitimate, but dismissing them with a passive excuse will not solve anything, and that way of thinking will get you stuck again. Whether it's the workplace expectations of the next generation, environmental responsibility, or something else, you've got to be constantly evolving with the times.

Keeping with our Millennial example, let's do what Nate did in chapter 1: approach the problem with curiosity, and look at *why* Millennials have different values from their predecessors.

In that same Gallup study I mentioned a moment ago, here is what those same respondents believe about the businesses they work for:

- Only 48 percent of respondents in a survey of 10,500 people believe corporations behave ethically.

9   Tejas Vemparala, "Why Millennials and Gen Z Change Jobs Often," Business News Daily, February 21, 2023, https://www.businessnewsdaily.com/7012-millennial-job-hopping.html.

10   Dawn Heiberg, "Key Statistics about Millennials in the Workplace," Firstup, October 26, 2021, https://firstup.io/blog/key-statistics-millennials-in-the-workplace/.

- A majority of Millennials across the world agree with the statement that businesses "have no ambition beyond wanting to make money."

This generation is fed up with organizations that only value their revenues and don't treat their employees or the environment with respect and appreciation. They are more informed, more educated, and more connected than any other generation, yet many of them cannot afford to purchase their own home, let alone make their way out of predatory student loan debt that was supposed to pay for itself in a well-earning job.

Millennials have seen that the Emperor has no clothes and are calling his bluff. Yet here you think because you offer a 1.25 percent cost of living raise, they should throw you a parade. Wake up. The workforce requires much more from their employers, and the mindset of "It's just business" isn't going to cut it. No wonder they are ready to leave the office by 5:00 p.m., especially considering that's when HR told them it closes.

> In comparison the companies that evolved with the times and are meeting the requests of Millennials see phenomenal results.

In comparison the companies that evolved with the times and are meeting the requests of Millennials see phenomenal results. The Gallup study also uncovered some incredible results organizations experience when they evolve with the times. Here is what they discovered about the companies that were rated by Millennials as the best places to work.

- When Millennials believe their company has a high-trust culture, they're more than twenty-two times more likely to want to work there for a long time.

- In comparison, Gen Xers are sixteen times more likely to want to stay, and Baby Boomers are thirteen times more likely.

- 88 percent of younger employees say they plan to stay long term at businesses considered "Best Workplaces for Millennials."

- At companies where managers show sincere interest in Millennials as people, the organization sees eight times improvement in agility and seven times increase in innovation.

It's not that Millennials don't want to work; they are ditching companies with toxic work cultures, who undervalue their employees or only focus on revenue. When they do land at a company that aligns with their values, they are fiercely loyal and bring innovative ideas to their roles, their teams, and the companies.

So if the problem isn't Millennials, it's the companies that refuse to evolve. *One of the key signs that you're being stodgy with your thinking is the unwillingness to consider that the problems could be internal.*

While we're using a very poignant example of employee retention and the values of Millennials, this can also apply to people from other generations as well as other departments. Think through your manufacturing, marketing, or any other area of your company that is facing a dilemma and ask yourself: *Are we struggling because we refuse to evolve with the times? How can we approach this issue with curiosity?*

STOP ACCEPTING CHEAP ANSWERS

One of the biggest indicators that you're getting stodgy in your thinking is how fast you are willing to accept what I like to call "cheap answers." A cheap answer is typically a dismissive excuse that magically explains away an issue without requiring any further research or change.

"It's these damn Millennials; they don't want to come into the office because they just don't want to work." This is the perfect example of a cheap answer. It automatically allows us to dismiss any underlying reasons for the problem or any responsibility to take part in resolving them. It preserves old ways of running your business, and doesn't require you to evolve with the times.

Cheap answers are often easy to spot as they don't hold up well with a little research. Sticking with our Millennial theme, let's peel back the layers and take a look at some data. We know from the previous stats that Millennials, especially when working for a great company, are highly valued members of their company teams and culture.

A similar study of Millennials by Gartner revealed, "When asked how they would prefer to schedule their work time, Millennials said they would spend the least amount of time in the office (<53 percent) when compared to Gen X (56 percent) and Baby Boomers (63 percent)." Younger people also shared that their top priorities when looking for a job are money (92 percent), security (87 percent), holidays/time off (86 percent), great people (80 percent), *and flexible working (79 percent)*. Additionally, employees that have adopted hybrid working environments and flexible work schedules are more productive and more efficient.[11]

It's not that Millennials don't want to work; they just don't want to spend their lives in an office. Millennials watched as their mothers, uncles, and fathers put in the long hours, hoping for the promotion

---

11   Katie Navarra. "In Hybrid Work, Don't Rely on Just One Aspect of Productivity," SHRM, October 9, 2022, https://www.shrm.org/resourcesandtools/hr-topics/employee-relations/pages/in-hybrid-work-dont-rely-on-just-one-aspect-of-productivity.aspx.

that, for many, never came. As productivity for their parents' and grandparents' generations increased, their wages did not keep pace.[12]

In traditional working hours, employees are expected to arrive at work by 8:00 a.m., and the day does not end until 5:00 p.m. Anyone who is looking for a promotion is expected to extend those hours and take on more responsibility, without any additional compensation. Then keep up that same exhausting pace once promoted.

Baby Boomers and many Gen Xers swallowed this philosophy full and sail. As a result, they literally disappeared from their personal lives to meet the unspoken expectations and "prove" themselves. The absence of those loved ones at the dinner table, baseball games, and recitals did not go unnoticed. Millennials had a front-row seat as the generations before sacrificed their mental and physical health along with any semblance of personal life, and they are simply unwilling to do the same. It's not that they don't want to work—they just also value autonomy, agency, and being fairly compensated for their work. The audacity.

With that revelatory information at hand, it's a little clearer to see why an answer like "these Millennials just don't want to work" is a cheap one. It protects your way of thinking and requires no responsibility on your part to evolve with the times. It's time to let go of your cheap answers.

Here are the signs that the answer you're arriving at is a cheap one:

- It's not supported by data.

- It values your opinion over another person's lived experience.

---

12   Lawrence Mishel, Elise Gould, and Josh Bivens, "Wage Stagnation in Nine Charts," Economic Policy Institute, https://www.epi.org/publication/charting-wage-stagnation/.

- It absolves you of any personal or professional responsibility to amend an infrastructure that you currently benefit from.

- It would add no value to the majority of the people who are affected by it.

Listen, cheap answers, in the long run, are exactly that…cheap. They cost you little and don't require much, if anything, from you. Yet in the long run, they are expensive. The cost is paid in the loss of talent, innovative solutions, and efficiency. You get what you pay for.

THE BEST IDEAS CAN BE AGELESS

One of the many gifts that I received from growing up in a multigenerational home was an appreciation for the unique perspective everyone brought to the table. My aunts, uncles, parents, and cousins learned so much from the wisdom and experience of my grandparents, whereas my grandparents benefited greatly from the fresh perspective that younger members of the family provided. Each generation brought something special to the table and the same perspective should be taken in your company.

Those that are considered "The Greatest Generation" (born between 1901 and 1927 and fought through World War II) possess a level of grit, and determination, that is hard to match. And on the other end of the spectrum, we have Gen Z, who are incredibly future focused and are leading the way when it comes to safeguarding our planet's resources and natural treasures. Whether it's a Baby Boomer, a Mil-

> **One of the many gifts that I received from growing up in a multigenerational home was an appreciation for the unique perspective everyone brought to the table.**

lennial, or in between, stop determining the value of someone's idea by their age or experience.

Listen, we've all been in a meeting with the intern who gives a naive answer, or the senior manager who spouts off an idea that reveals that they are out of touch. People are still people, you are going to be flawed at any age. That doesn't mean you should discount someone's input because of when they were born.

No matter someone's age, they are capable of generating fantastic ideas that could benefit your organization and empower you to evolve with the times. By creating a safe environment where everyone's contributions are valued, your team will continue to improve, and when the day comes that they have a great idea, they won't be afraid to share it. The moment you start shaming them for their naivete or their "old" way of thinking is the moment they will stop contributing, making it much more difficult for you to evolve with the times.

> By creating a safe environment where everyone's contributions are valued, your team will continue to improve, and when the day comes that they have a great idea, they won't be afraid to share it.

INVOLVE THE NEXT GENERATION

While apprenticeships are no longer commonplace, it was once the only way to learn a trade. An apprentice is defined as someone who is learning by practical experience under skilled workers in a trade, art, or calling. An apprenticeship was a much more in-depth and comprehensive approach than what the standard internship offers. An apprentice would shadow and study a "master" while at work in their craft, but also as they ran their business, absorbing how to negotiate with the other trades and the practicalities of supply and demand. Eventually, when a master would retire, the apprentices would take over the business. It was a beautiful way to hire the help you need, empower the next generation, and continue to keep your business relevant with a fresh perspective.

While in many businesses apprenticeships have fallen out of fashion, it provides an amazing blueprint on how to raise up the next generation of managers and leaders in our companies.

Not long ago my coaching client, Alyssa, was a twenty-five-year-old college grad with no clue what she wanted to do with her career. Like many young people who are launching careers, she was struggling with that age-old dilemma, *what do I want to be when I grow up?*

After sharing her struggles with her mother and stepfather, Joe, he offered her an entry-level job in the finance department of his company. It was a good plan for everyone; Alyssa could get some work experience as she explored her options and the short-staffed department would get a needed set of hands from an educated and capable team member. Everyone assumed Alyssa would find a more permanent job someplace else in a year or two, and that would be that. But that is not where our story ends.

Alyssa was a breath of fresh air. Her natural ability to wrangle numbers and her amazing people skills immediately made her an all-star in the finance department. She was quickly promoted and it was not long before she was running the entire department. Her untapped potential did not go unnoticed and, just as the trades would with their apprentices in the days of old, Joe began inviting Alyssa to sit in on client and leadership meetings. Eventually, Joe began to casually ask for her thoughts and opinions on various matters. He was consistently impressed by her keen business instincts, as well as her ability to read a room and know exactly how to manage a conversation.

A few years passed and, eventually, Joe began to look toward his future and retirement. Based on what he had seen over the past five years, he knew Alyssa had the potential to take on the CEO role. While she lacked the technical experience Joe knew she was the right one, as, over the years, he had been slowly evaluating the various department managers, but none of them seemed to be a good fit. After watching Alyssa run her department and expertly navigate several client meetings, in his mind it was settled. She had what it took to run this company and carry it into the future. She was a force to be reckoned with, and, Joe realized, the future of the company.

It's tempting to not involve the younger people in meetings that are "above their pay grade." And it's very true that in the beginning, they may not understand the complexities or nuances of your industry, but they will never learn if they are not exposed. On the flip side, by not including younger blood, those meetings can often become stale and frustrating. Without the infusion of new perspective, you will become increasingly stuck, eventually irrelevant, and have no one to leave your legacy to.

> I'd like to suggest that instead of asking people to climb the ladder, let's shift our approach to inviting them to join us on the boat.

In corporate culture, we've become obsessed with the idea that someone should have to climb the corporate ladder. And from everything I can see, it's really not serving us well. The ladder automatically places us in a mindset of isolation and fierce competition. I'd like to suggest that instead of asking people to climb the ladder, let's shift our approach to inviting them to join us on the boat.

Think about it, sailing requires so much more than hard work. For all involved, it demands cooperation, teamwork, trust, and a willingness to learn from one another. The same is true for your company. The failure to incorporate this approach will result in you getting stuck in your ways, alienated and with no one left to take the helm when you're ready to retire.

Begin treating your employees as apprentices rather than minions who are simply meant to do your bidding. They will keep you young, your perspective fresh, and be your saving grace when it's time to chart the course forward.

Questions from the Vault

1. What cheap answers have you been accepting? How will you begin to challenge the idea?

2. What can you do to encourage everyone, no matter their age, to volunteer new ideas and solutions?

3. Name two younger people in your company you can begin treating as an apprentice and inviting them to higher level meetings and discussions?

CHAPTER EIGHT

Learning How to Pivot

"YOUR CHOICE, TODAY AND IN THE FUTURE, IS TO PIVOT OR GET PIVOTED. PIVOTING IS A MINDSET AND A SKILL SET, AND YOU CAN GET BETTER AT BOTH."

—JENNY BLAKE, PIVOT

In 2012, Derek Ball and Ben Brannen founded atVenu, a point-of-sale software that would soon revolutionize the live event and music industry. At the time, many musicians, music festivals, and other live events were managing their merchandise stocks and processing payments through a hodgepodge of spreadsheets, the internal systems of managers (or interns), and systems such as PayPal. And while everyone was perfectly happy with the system as it was, clearly there was an untapped market ready for a tech solution.

When atVenu launched services it was revolutionary. With this one app, artists were now able to track all merchandise sales, keep tabs on stock in multiple locations, automatically generate sales reports, and easily submit vital information to their labels, accountants, and management teams. All of this was wrapped in a user-friendly interface, and accounts were only charged for the service if they had a show that month.

While in many ways atVenu was an artist's dream come true, it was slow to be adopted in the music industry. On-site merchandise managers who had spent years perfecting their spreadsheets, and who didn't trust the system's ability to keep an accurate tally of stocks, were hesitant to try atVenu. Additionally, large name labels, like Sony or Warner Music, are famously slow in adopting new systems and they especially did not want to rock the boat when it came to tracking record sales at live events.

Slowly but surely one band or manager after another would adopt atVenu and was quickly won over by its easy design and flawless functionality. "Have you tried atVenu?" soon became the point of conversation in tour planning and album sales strategy meetings. Even with the streamlined tracking, artists still were required to submit their official album sales numbers the old-fashioned way, with pen and paper and a signature from the hosting venue, or promoter, as well as the artist.

Then everything changed practically overnight. atVenu announced a collaboration with the main reporting and tracking system for album sales, Nielsen SoundScan. Artists and labels were now able to seamlessly submit and track all album sales digitally. These numbers determine which albums end up in your top one hundred, top ten lists, and also when an album has reached the coveted gold or platinum status in sales. So to say they are important would be a bit of an understatement.

Suddenly every major label was requiring their artists to sign up for atVenu and footing the cost for the basic membership that included submissions of SoundScan reports. With that one small pivot, atVenu took off and has since become the standard in live event point-of-sale systems and merchandise management. Not just for artists but festivals and just about any live event you can think of. The start-up now manages well over one hundred thousand shows annually from small clubs to stadium events.

From the software company making the pivot to include submissions of album sales to the artists who adopted the revolutionary system for managing their income streams, the atVenu story is a perfect example of why every business must stay open to pivoting. Oftentimes it's the smallest pivots that can be the biggest game changers in your business.

While many CEOs will say they are willing to embrace change, like the musicians, we are often slow or even cynical of the opportunities when they present themselves. The ability to pivot is a skill that can be learned and cultivated, so that when those previous opportunities present themselves, you can adopt them before it's too late.

> Oftentimes it's the smallest pivots that can be the biggest game changers in your business.

KEEP IN TOUCH

One of the best ways you can develop your ability to pivot is by staying in constant communication with other leaders, both in and outside of your industry. This is why I recommend every CEO join a confidential coaching group such as the one I host, Vistage International, which is in thirty-five countries, with forty-five thousand members and six hundred chairs, comprised of elite leaders who help CEOs, business owners, and key executives reach their highest potential. If you're ripe with indignation at the suggestion you openly share with other CEOs, you're not the first. While leadership lends itself to isolation, many CEOs choose to stay completely insulated, fearful that someone would steal their secret recipe to success.

That thinking is often shortsighted and leads to self-sabotage. Believing you can tackle it all on your own is at the root of what caused you to get stuck in the first place. The CEOs who join and participate in the group coaching sessions often come to view our monthly meetings as a lifeline. It's one of the few places where they can share both their challenges and triumphs without judgment or criticism.

There are so many advantages to keeping in close communication and up to speed with other CEOs. You have the chance to learn and grow from the experiences your colleagues are facing, allowing you to give and receive unbiased feedback and gain valuable outside perspective. Additionally, it allows you to keep your ear to the ground so you can be in the know when it comes to new technologies and trends that could benefit your company. Lastly, it helps to normalize the pivoting process and just how often it's necessary. No company, even the ones that are successful from the jump, can stay the same forever and survive.

> Believing you can tackle it all on your own is at the root of what caused you to get stuck in the first place.

The cross-pollination of ideas and opportunities for fresh perspective from joining and staying in touch with a peer group of CEOs is truly invaluable and will make the opportunities to pivot and grow a lot less scary.

DON'T GET COMFORTABLE NOW

The main reason CEOs or companies struggle to pivot is they have mistook their comfort for safety. In the case of atVenu, many artists and merchandise managers and the industry as a whole were comfortable with the hodgepodge system of various spreadsheets, waiting days on end for reports and accepting the uncertainty that came with miscounting of merchandise. In an industry where word-of-mouth referral is the lifeblood of how anything happens, a brand-new software system that no one had any experience with was terrifying.

> Yes change is risky, but you are also taking a risk when you choose *not* to change.

The same can be said for many businesses. We get comfortable with the current way of doing things, our process, and the team dynamic and accepting of a certain margin of error. So when the opportunity to expand, explore, or take a fresh approach is presented it is at worst terrifying and at best inconvenient. Why risk it?

Whether we have been in business five days or fifty years, you have to accept that everything comes with a risk. Yes change is risky, but you are also taking a risk when you choose *not* to change. You're better off risking and failing, then doing nothing and eventually fading into obscurity.

NEVER SAY NEVER

If black swan events like the sinking of the Titanic, 9/11, or the COVID-19 pandemic have taught us anything, it's to never say never.

Yet it still amazes me how we continue to underestimate how the smallest changes can create the biggest upsets.

I experienced my own David and Goliath story in 1996 and I was considering purchasing a small, mom-and-pop Harley-Davidson dealership in the historical town of St. Augustine in northeast Florida. Nestled between Jacksonville, the largest city in land mass in the country, and Daytona, the host of the Daytona Bike Week, which is the world's largest motorcycle event, I thought there was no way this little shop in a tiny tourist town would be able to compete.

Despite my skepticism, I was in the business of buying dealerships, so I at least wanted to do my due diligence, run the numbers, and scout the place out. As I passed by one Sunday afternoon, I saw the beachside shop's parking lot was overflowing with bikes and the picnic tables out-front hosting close to a dozen bikers. Since the shop was closed on Sundays, I was intrigued and pulled in.

As I struck up a conversation with the bikers, I was shocked to learn that none of them were from St. Augustine but instead from Jacksonville and Daytona. As most were busy professionals the weekend was the only time they had to enjoy their motorcycles and so they would hop on the scenic A1A oceanfront highway and head in the direction of St. Augustine.

In that moment, I knew this store could be a roaring success and immediately made an offer. I began to cater to and build relationships with the weekend riders. Barbecuing at the shop and serving lunch on Saturdays was a huge draw for them to stop into the shop and peruse our inventory. And while we remained closed on Sunday in deference to the original owners, I expanded and updated the seating area out-front for the Sunday crowd, who were amazed that I still wanted to serve them even when they weren't purchasing.

Soon a loyal customer base began to grow exponentially as the riders would intentionally bring their business to my small shop in St. Augustine and forgo the convenience of their local Harley shop. Both the Jacksonville and Daytona dealerships were in shock as they never thought that the small mom-and-pop shop would ever provide them with any real competition.

All because I had learned to never say never, and be open to a small pivot that could create a huge change.

Questions from the Vault

1. What new software or industry trend have you been avoiding? Could a pivot in that direction be beneficial?

2. When was the last time you received unbiased advice from a colleague? Who is someone you could call today and ask for a fresh perspective?

PART THREE
Crafting Your Legacy

One of the biggest mistakes I see CEOs make is their inability to consider their legacy as they build their empires. You have to begin with the end in mind. As they move toward retirement and the late third of their life, they then find themselves asking, what was it all for? You are in a unique position as you are still actively captaining your ship, but you must understand, this work you're doing is all for nothing if you leave no greater impact after you're gone. Spanning the gap between simply success and leaving a legacy is one that requires intentionality and curiosity in both your personal and professional life. How do you press forward when you face devastating setbacks? What do you do after you've checked off all the boxes of success? These questions are just the beginning as we begin to explore what it means to craft a legacy you can be proud of.

CHAPTER NINE
Dust Yourself Off
and Keep Going

In a culture that often praises meteoric rises, and seemingly overnight success, it can be easy to forget that the road to leadership is a long one. Big-name CEOs like Bezos or Zuckerberg, who had an idea that took off relatively quickly, create the sense that once you've reached "the top," you're untouchable. Yet the truth is a lot less sexy. You're going to face setbacks, big ones, and only the leaders who learn to dust themselves off and keep going are the ones who can create something truly impactful and leave a legacy.

Success in business is often painted like a true love fairy tale. Once we reach the C-suite position or our business breaks the seven-figure mark, we believe we'll ride off into the sunset to live happily ever after. An endless stream of year over year growth, and challenging yet fulfilling day in the office, when in truth, the journey of business looks more like a two-part race. The first part of the race consists of a climb to the top of Mount Kilimanjaro, and once you do, the second part is a 200-mile ultra-marathon.

Climbing to the C-suite position or making your first seven figures is summiting Mount Kilimanjaro. It's a climb that takes endurance and discipline, but you do so with the promise that you'll reach the top. Yet the actual *running* of a successful business day to day, year in and year out, is the 200-mile ultra-marathon that follows. Marathons require a different kind of endurance, and patience. There is no shortcut, only the consistency of tackling each mile's challenges as it comes.

> You're going to face setbacks, big ones, and only the leaders who learn to dust themselves off and keep going are the ones who can create something truly impactful and leave a legacy.

While everyone prepares for the initial climb, very few prepare for part two, the marathon. They are then caught off guard when they come face to face with the unavoidable truth of marathons, not every mile is a great one. And so it goes, not every quarter or year will be a great one for your business. Just as a marathon runner must accept that blisters and getting stuck behind someone at a slower pace are part of the race, you must accept that both internal and external struggles will occur.

While these setbacks are unpreventable, they are never insurmountable. Like a runner, you can use best practices to minimize the fallout, strategize your next steps, and come back stronger. But above all, you must resolve within yourself that giving up is not an option and that no matter what comes your way, you can dust yourself off and keep going.

FACING A TOXIC WORK ENVIRONMENT

There is nothing worse than trying to lead within a company that has developed a toxic work environment. In these companies where the culture is toxic, oftentimes the communication is poor, trust is low, and burnout is commonplace. Overall, the negative atmosphere makes it difficult for employees to complete their work or advance their careers. Unfortunately, in a poll of five hundred workers, across eleven different industries, a stunning 87 percent of partici-pants report having worked in a toxic environment.[13] To go back to our analogy of being a captain of a ship, if your engine room employees are always exhausted and feel unappreciated, and your crew on the bridge is constantly sabotaging each other, you can imagine that it can be tough to get where you need to go.

> You must resolve within yourself that giving up is not an option and that no matter what comes your way, you can dust yourself off and keep going.

---

13   Shelby Palmeri, "2022 Toxic Work Environment Report: What It Is and How to Fix It," CareerPlug, June 27, 2022, https://www.careerplug.com/blog/toxic-work-environment/.

IDENTIFY THE BIGGEST CAUSAL FACTOR

A toxic work environment tends to have a splintering effect. So while there may be several issues that must be addressed—high turnover, micromanaging, underperforming, etc.—they are the effects, not the cause. Typically these causes of toxic work culture start at the top, which means the problem is either you or the board.

We'll start with the board members; it's an easier pill to swallow. Boards can be incredibly helpful as they provide a wealth of resources and information. I have also seen boards that were over-demanding, heavily critical, and left CEOs incredibly frustrated. The CEO then passes on their sense of frustration to the rest of the company. If this sounds familiar, and you're struggling with your board, your best bet is to find ways to get them on your side. Push back without being combative by asking questions in response to their demands or criticisms. This invites board members to become part of the solutions and can often illuminate the inherent issues in their demands. From there, you can propose realistic solutions and timelines that won't leave your workforce struggling.

If the problem is not the board, the next place you need to look to address the source of a toxic work environment is *you*. Unfortunately, this requires a level of self-awareness that not many CEOs possess. Remember our friend Taylor from chapter 6, who insisted on micromanaging all forty of his employees? To this day, I am sad to say that Taylor still is confounded by the incredible amount of turnover his company experiences year in and year out. Also, it's important to take into account that studies have shown that over 70 percent of

Americans have experienced trauma in their life.[14] This means many CEOs are leading their companies from a place of trauma.

While you may or may not have unresolved trauma, the problem is simple: Either you are the genesis of the toxic work environment or have allowed one to grow under your watch.

That being the case, the best thing you can do is what my mother used to preach to my brothers and me: accept the blame and assume that you're the problem. Only then can you be the source of the solution. Take responsibility for the problem so you can get to work fixing it. A toxic work environment is like a leaky roof; the real damage is done when you sit back and do nothing.

FIND ONE WAY TO MOVE THE BALL DOWN THE COURT

Often in toxic work environments, it's difficult to get anything done, let alone address the subsequent issues. This can be incredibly disheartening when trying to implement systemic change. Whether you're facing bureaucracy or a slow to adapt team, try implementing just one solution at a time. While this won't cause the culture to shift 180 degrees overnight, it will slowly but surely move the ball down the court.

The tech giant Shopify recently accomplished this when in one fell swoop, they canceled all company meetings that had more than two people attending, the goal being to give their employees time back

---

14   Corina Benjet et al., "The Epidemiology of Traumatic Event Exposure Worldwide: Results from the World Mental Health Survey Consortium," NCBI, October 29, 2015, https://www.ncbi.nlm.nih.gov/pmc/articles/PMC4869975/.

to accomplish their work. In that one simple decision, the result was deleting nearly ten thousand events, and clearing up 76,500 hours![15]

Just imagine what a difference that made in the daily lives of each employee at Shopify, where they actually have the ability to do their work, instead of sitting in meetings all day. Never underestimate the impact of one change.

WHAT HAPPENS WHEN YOU'RE FIRED?

While no one plans to get fired, it happens more often than you would think. It does not matter if you're the CEO or even if you helped found the company, getting fired is part of business. I have been fired three times in the course of my career, yet the time I was ousted from American Power Sports, which I had built from the ground up, was the one that stung the most. The experience left me reeling and asking myself, "My God, what do I do next?"

As I shared previously, I founded American Power Sports, where, with the backing of a private equity company, I bought and turned around struggling power sports dealerships. We were one of the first to adopt this model of business, and in only eight years, I had built the company up to grossing over $200 million in revenue.

I had a great relationship with the board of directors, so I was a little shocked when two of them abruptly flew to Nashville to have dinner with me. Over the course of the evening, they made it clear they were unhappy with my plan for the upcoming year and the smaller purchases I proposed. The board wanted to see the same exponential growth I had delivered in those first couple of years to satiate

---

15 Jennifer Korn, "This Tech Company Is Clearing Out Recurring Meetings from Employee Calendars," CNN, January 3, 2023, https://www.cnn.com/2023/01/03/tech/shopify-meetings/index.html.

investors' constant need to see a compounded return on their invest-ment. I pushed back; in my experience, that kind of rapid growth is ultimately unsustainable. I was in ultra-marathon mode and was, in many ways, playing the long game after the initial success of those first years.

During dinner, the board members seemingly conceded to my long-term strategy and prudent approach to growth. Still, I left with an uneasy feeling; my gut knew something was up, but I did my best to shake it off.

Surprise, surprise, my gut was right. Two weeks later, I received a call informing me I would be discharged from my position as CEO. At first, I was deeply hurt and incredibly discouraged. While I knew this was one of the risks of partnering with a private equity firm, it still stings when you are ousted from the business you built from the ground up.

As news spread throughout the industry and to my colleagues, something happened that completely changed my perspective. I received no less than a dozen phone calls from people congratulating me! Some were colleagues who had experienced the headaches that come with partnering with a private equity firm. Still, most were from other executives and entre-preneurs who had also been fired over the course of their career. Each of them shared a story of how getting fired served as a springboard launching them on to their greatest career triumphs.

Being terminated can be one of the best things to happen to your career. It gives you permission to

> Being terminated can be one of the best things to happen to your career. It gives you permission to once again take risks, become inventive, and reimagine what your life could look like without the fear of what you may lose.

once again take risks, become inventive, and reimagine what your life could look like without the fear of what you may lose. And for me, this certainly was the case. This change in employment was my springboard to launch my executive coaching business, a career I would never have considered before, yet employs all my strengths, talents, and experience, while empowering other CEOs to do the same!

Yes, getting fired is a setback, but it's exactly that, a setback. It's not the end. When your number is drawn, and it happens to most of us at least once in our careers, don't rush into another role to simply have one. Take some time, connect with friends and loved ones, and determine what it is you really want. In this space, you have an opportunity to dream and ask questions, and that is where the good stuff happens.

TRUST YOUR GUT

When setbacks occur, like getting fired, a poor sales report, or a client rejection, we easily question ourselves and our abilities. Just like ultra-marathon runners who experience blisters, muscle cramps, or a particularly challenging terrain, you wonder, "Do I really have what it takes to run this race?" Setbacks are part of the journey but become game-enders when they cause us to question our gut. In the midst of setbacks, it's more important than ever to stick to your values and trust your intuition.

In the early stages of career or business growth, you have that Mount Kilimanjaro certainty. You know in your gut that you're going to reach the top, and it helps you to manifest your goals. To a certain extent, you rose to your current level of success because you followed your intuition and were able to bring your vision to reality.

Unfortunately, nothing will cause you to doubt your intuition more than a setback. In the shadow of a setback, we often turn to data to guide us. And while data can be important, if the only tool we had to build careers on was a mound of data of the thousands of people who tried and failed, no one would ever attempt anything significant.

It's important to remember that intuition is not the absence of data; far from it. World-renowned researcher and scientist Dr. Brené Brown powerfully describes intuition as "not a single way of knowing—it's our ability to hold space for uncertainty and our willingness to trust the many ways we've developed knowledge and insight, including instinct, experience, faith, and reason."[16] We've all had a moment when data told us one thing but something deep inside, our gut, if you will, told us differently. This combination of reason and instinct is what allows us to imagine unforeseen solutions and innovate a new path forward.

This combination of reason and instinct is what allows us to imagine unforeseen solutions and innovate a new path forward.

So as you look to dust yourself off and chart a path forward, yes, learn from your previous mistakes but fold them into that intuition that will convert your vision into a reality; when you lay your head down at night, you know whether or not you're making the right choice.

---

16 Brené Brown, *The Gifts of Imperfection* (Center City, Minnesota: Hazelden Publishing, 2010).

Questions from the Vault

1. Think of the toxic characteristics of your company's work culture that are causing stress and tension for employees. What is *one thing* you can do to bring change to this area?

2. If you were fired today and tomorrow could start over completely fresh, what would you dream of doing? Is there any way you can incorporate that idea into what you are doing today?

3. Identify one area of the business where you have not been trusting your gut and it's beginning to eat away at you. What is one actionable step you can take in the next thirty days to bring that area back into alignment with your intuition?

CHAPTER TEN
What Happens after Success?

As I stepped onto the campus of Trevecca University, I double-checked the name of the building and the room number I was looking for. At fifty years old most of the students assumed I was there as an instructor. Almost three decades after graduating with my bachelor's degree, I was finally going back to school for my MBA. Not because I needed the credential on my résumé or because I believed there was a gaping hole in my knowledge of how businesses work—I was fulfilling a lifelong dream.

Higher education has always been immensely important in my family. My older brother held a PhD and I always stressed to my sons the importance of education. In 1968, when I graduated with my bachelor's, I immediately applied to law school and was accepted. At the same time I received my acceptance letter, I also was handed a job offer from Chrysler. While I felt torn, I reasoned that long term, the plan was always to work in the automotive industry and decided to take the job.

Despite knowing my decision was a good one and experiencing a steady rise through the ranks of Chrysler, the dream of obtaining a master's was never far from my mind. During slow seasons at work, or in a moment of solitude, I would find myself asking "Is now the time? Should I go for it and register to go back to school?" Each time I told myself that I was successfully climbing the corporate ladder without a master's degree, so why bother? Then in 1995 life threw me another curve ball, as it tends to do, and I was fired from my role as COO at Mazda. The reasons I was dismissed were not necessarily due to my performance. The new CEO and I did not see eye to eye, which ultimately made me a bad fit for the position. You can have all the skills and experience in the world but if you are not a good fit with the team it's never going to work. It's not necessarily anyone's fault.

As word spread about my parting ways with Mazda, the job offers began to roll in. Thanks to my deep connections and over two decades of steady performance, I was in demand. The chance to pursue success for the sake of success was there. But something inside of me knew now was the time to go back to school. I didn't want to get another twenty years down the road and still wish I had taken the opportunity to pursue something deeply rewarding. Up until then, my entire professional experience had been with Chrysler and Mazda; I had made it to the top of the ladder and found myself wondering, well, what's next?

So I signed up for classes, and for the next two years, I was happy to be "the old guy" in each class. I could feel parts of my brain light up as I learned the newest approaches and systems. My perspective widened as I heard the answers and ideas of my classmates that were two and three decades my junior but intellectually my peer.

Many CEOs have arrived at the same crossroad I did. You get to the place where you've checked off all of the prescribed boxes of "success," and suddenly you wonder, could there be more? The idea of simply rinsing and repeating has lost its appeal. While I love the automotive industry and was making plans to dive back in, I was coming to understand that I needed more from life than simply being "successful." I wanted to consider what it would look like to create a rich life outside of business goals and a deeper impact than a record-breaking quarter. For me, the first step was fulfilling a lifelong dream of obtaining my master's degree and obtaining my MBA.

There is more to life than simply being "successful," but for most of us, we were raised and instructed that it's the only thing that matters. So we're left asking, "What happens after success?" While what would define a rich and fulfilling life is as unique as every individual, the key is to listen to the longing inside of you, that gut instinct, and not be afraid to follow it. For me it has always been wanting to be the best example to my two sons.

IT'S TIME TO FIND YOUR WHY OUTSIDE OF DOLLAR SIGNS

In my coaching practice, I repeatedly find myself discussing with my clients their "why." When Simon Sinek published his bestselling book *Start with Why* in 2009, he changed the internal landscape of many companies as he issued the call that companies can not only focus on what they are selling but on *why* they sell it. When it comes to a company's long-term strategic planning and day-to-day operations, centering the "why" can make a huge impact on the decisions you make and the direction you take the ship. While many CEOs can easily enough apply this principle to their company as a whole, they seldom take the extra step of defining their personal "why." Then they wonder why they find themselves surrounded by success but feel completely unfulfilled.

Remember our friend Nate back in chapter 1, who took his company from nothing to $100 million in revenue in five years? In chapter 1, I outlined the amazing programs Nate had piloted to address the underlying issues that were preventing his staff from coming to work on time or no-show quitting; before those plans were in place, he was under an immense amount of stress and pressure. Biggie was not lying; with more money comes more problems.

In his book *Start with Why*, Sinek explains, "Knowing your WHY is not the only way to be successful, but it is the only way to maintain a lasting success and have a greater blend of innovation and flexibility. When a WHY goes fuzzy, it becomes much more difficult to maintain the growth, loyalty, and inspiration that helped drive the original success. By difficult, I mean that manipulation rather than inspiration fast become the strategy of choice to motivate behavior. This is effective in the short term but comes at a high cost in the long term."[17]

For many of us, myself included, the original goal of going into business was to be as financially successful as possible. I'm also a second-generation American. I was raised on the stories of grandparents who sacrificed all they knew so that their children could lead a "better life," and I understood the phrase "better life" meant financial success. While financial success is not in and of itself a bad why, money can only take you so far.

Since becoming a coach, I've seen a steady stream of financially successful CEOs, who struggle to sleep at night and feel trapped by the very company they've built. They live their daily lives constantly running from fire to fire with no end in sight. Yes, they are "successful," but maintaining the success feels like pushing the boat rather than captaining a ship.

Nate's original goal was to make money, and since then has made more in five years than most men make in five lifetimes. He could have sold off his company, been done with the headaches, and lived out his life on a lake house somewhere. He would never have to worry again about staffing the warehouse. So, what was the point of staying? That's when his "why" comes in. Recently in our peer group coaching session, Nate shared with his fellow CEOs, "My purpose now is to make sure every single one of those 3,000 employees has a job when they wake up

> When you understand your why, it serves as a North Star, providing focus and guidance on approaching an issue or accomplishing your goals.

---

17   Simon Sinek, *Start with Why: How Great Leaders Inspire Everyone to Take Action* (New York, New York: Penguin Publishing Group, 2009).

tomorrow." Born from that deeper purpose were the solutions to his staffing issue.

When you understand your why, it serves as a North Star, providing focus and guidance on approaching an issue or accomplishing your goals. My why centered around my two boys and the life I wanted to give them. I dreamed of providing them a chance to see the world, take road trips with their dad, and attend an excellent university without fear of paying for it.

By defining a deeper purpose than financial gain, you forge the path to a rich and fulfilling life, one that frees you up to have deeper relationships, meaningful experiences, and a legacy of positive impact.

WHAT DO YOU WANT YOUR ROLE TO LOOK LIKE?

While we've already stressed the importance of building a successful team, as your company grows, you will need to continually empower that team with more responsibility. When a ship captain has an experienced and trustworthy crew, there is ease to the hard work. He doesn't need to micromanage the engine room or constantly look over the shoulder of his navigational officer. In fact, he should have more time and energy to step away as well as focus on the work of setting the destination.

Between industry changes and projected growth, your business will never cease to evolve. For many CEOs, it's difficult to break the habit of taking on new responsibilities or roles as the company expands. This is why you must continue to reevaluate your roles, and the parts your team members play, and continue to delegate. It's simply not enough to do it only once.

In line with delegating, the more your company grows the more time off you should be taking. You simply cannot pour out from an empty cup, and in order to recharge you have to step away. As you continually reevaluate your role, you should consistently be asking, "What do I need to pass off so that I can reasonably step away on vacation a couple of times a year?"

Maybe you stop attending those meetings that the department head can attend for you. Perhaps it's passing off all your scheduling to your executive assistant because

> The more your company grows the more time off you should be taking.

you know they will honor boundaries that you won't. Whatever it is, know that delegating and continuing to stay out of the weeds is what's going to keep you in the game.

CULTIVATE A RICH PERSONAL LIFE

Success means nothing if you do not have a life you enjoy outside of your computer screen. There are plenty of millionaires out there who have passed away and nobody remembers them. Sure they may remember what they did for work, or that they had a lot of money, but they were never truly known as human beings. That is a legacy that no one wants to leave. When looking to cultivate a rich personal life it's important to develop meaningful relationships, find a hobby you enjoy, and prioritize your health.

Develop Meaningful Relationships

In *The Good Life: Lessons from the World's Longest Scientific Study of Happiness*, Dr. Robert Waldinger and Dr. Marc Schulz answer a question that people have been asking for thousands of years. The seventy-five-year research study shows that the key to a good life, a fulfilling and happy life, is meaningful relationships. Waldinger explains, "It turns out that people who are more socially connected to family, to friends, to community, are happier, they're physically healthier, and they live longer than people who are less well connected."[18]

Yes, we can have wonderful and meaningful experiences on our own, but what makes a fulfilling *life* is the people we spend it with. Think about it. When you reflect on some of the most treasured moments of your life up until now, I would bet good money that most, if not all of them, were made more special by the people you experience them with. Whether it was the day your child was born, the vacation of your dreams, or a rich moment from a holiday celebration, it's the people who we spend our lives with that bring a depth of meaning that we cannot achieve on our own.

> It's the people who we spend our lives with that bring a depth of meaning that we cannot achieve on our own.

Take a look around the landscape of your life and see if you can name three or five people whom you live in authentic and honest community with. Sure, your spouse or partner can be one, but they should not be the *only* one; that is too much for anyone to handle. Work should not be an excuse for having deep relationships because everything you are working for is worthless if you do not have loved ones to share it with.

---

18   Robert Waldinger and Marc Schulz, *The Good Life: Lessons from the World's Longest Scientific Study of Happiness* (New York, New York: Simon & Schuster, 2023).

Find a Hobby

When was the last time you engaged with something that did not generate income or wasn't a social obligation? If you're struggling to find an answer then it's time to explore a hobby. Maybe it's playing a round of golf, taking up pottery, or trying an improv class; the possibilities are endless. And honestly, it doesn't matter what your hobby is, simply that you have one.

Having a hobby is proven to improve your mental health, strengthen relationships, and lower your stress level. Many CEOs are perfectionists and productivity addicts, so the idea of taking part in something that we may not excel at or doesn't produce a "result" is off-putting. Unfortunately, if you want a life you truly love, where you enjoy your success, you will have to get over it. You're a human *being*, not a human *doing*. Create space to simply be, explore, and try something you could enjoy.

Prioritize Your Mental, Physical, and Spiritual Health

I get it, when you're stressed, busy, and have people depending on you, the first thing that gets pushed to the back burner is your health. We say things like, "I'll sleep when I'm dead" as an easy way out. We think it makes us look more important and that there will be time down the road.

News flash, you are not promised tomorrow. You're not promised a retirement where you can learn how to play tennis and go for long runs. You're not promised another Easter, Rosh Hashanah, or Eid Mubarak to get your butt back to the church, synagogue, mosque, or whatever place of worship you've been holding off visiting. And there is definitely no guarantee that your loved ones will wait years on end for you to take yourself to therapy and work your crap out. Don't wait; begin to prioritize your physical, mental, and spiritual health today!

Over the years, I've had a handful of clients who truly had very little semblance of a personal life outside of their work, and a select few have no desire for any. When I think of these CEOs, it's always with a twinge of sadness. From an outside perspective, I can see the effect this has on both their employees and on them as a human. They often expect their employees to keep the same round-the-clock schedule that they adhere to, unable to see that it eventually results in unhappy employees and crappy work. In their personal lives, it's saddening because I know what they are missing out on—a level of fulfillment and contentment that no KPI can fulfill.

Questions from the Vault

1. When considering your personal why, what comes to mind? What would change if you began to live your life and run your company with your why in mind?

2. Think through the changes that have happened in your company in the last year. What roles and responsibilities have you taken on that need to be passed off to someone else on your leadership team?

3. List three to five relationships that are meaningful to you. What have you done lately to pour into that relationship?

CHAPTER ELEVEN
Surviving Growth

Many people innately understand that launching or founding a business is a big lift, but only some realize growth can often be even more arduous. So when the opportunity for expansion comes around, they are caught off guard when it is difficult.

Never assume that as your company grows, the process will become easier. Plan for change to be uncomfortable and reward your employees accordingly. Additionally, your exit plan should always be front-of-mind in each phase of your growth. This is why you must refrain from ever assuming that, as your company grows, the process will become easier. There is simply never any phase of running a company where everything is going to run smoothly. Luckily, there are a few tried-and-tested strategies that will make surviving growth a little smoother.

RETAIN AND REWARD YOUR GOLD EMPLOYEES

After being on maternity leave for the past twelve weeks, Anna excitedly sat down with her CEO, David, for lunch. While she was thankful for the time to connect with her new baby and heal from delivery, she was excited to return to work at a job and a company she loved. Anna had been working for David for the past three years at his small artist management agency in Nashville, Tennessee. Within the first year, Anna had taken on managing the day-to-day operations of the company and speaking into the strategy behind each of their client's careers. Also, in that three-year window, David's company experienced explosive growth; in large part, he credited Anna, who was instrumental in managing the growth and empowering David to do his best work.

Before she left on maternity leave, David and Anna confirmed that they would reevaluate Anna's role to reflect her amazing contributions and account for her new lifestyle changes. They were both eager for her to return to work.

As they sipped their coffee, David began, "Anna, your absence the past couple of months has truly highlighted the value you bring to the company and our clients. While the team has done a good job of holding down the fort, it has been quite illuminating to see what we've been missing out on, especially the ease in which everything happens when you're present and managing the day-to-day operations."

Anna was elated to hear David's words of encouragement. She was coming into the discussion with a few big requests but hearing how much she was appreciated and valued made her feel more confident.

"When you return in a few weeks," David continued, "I'd like to propose that we officially give you the title of COO. I want to completely hand off all the day-to-day operations and let you work your magic without my approval or input unless you request it. Additionally, I would like to hire another person under your team so you have the support you need as the company continues to grow."

Anna was overwhelmed by David's kind words and offer. While she had hoped to grow within the company and industry, the official title and offer to expand her team were more than what she was hoping for. The past three years of riding out the company's growth were difficult for Anna. When she started at the company, she saw it as a rare opportunity to expand her skills and work in a place where her unique talents would be appreciated. While the salary and position were far from ideal, she was willing to "pay her dues" and prove herself.

"Thank you, David," Anna responded graciously, "it has definitely been a wild ride the past couple of years, but I have loved almost every minute. I'm excited to explore this new role you're creating for me, and I feel like my talents are truly appreciated. May I ask what you envision for the salary compensation?"

A look of surprise momentarily crossed David's face, and Anna felt a pit start to form in her stomach. "Well..." David began slowly, "my thought was that we could continue with your current salary. As you know, we have an unlimited PTO policy which I feel is a huge benefit in our industry, but," he paused, "I'm open to hearing what you are thinking."

While Anna was unnerved to hear that David had not been considering any sort of increase in financial compensation, she had come prepared to negotiate. She had accurately researched what competing companies were compensating similar employees and spoken with trusted professionals in the industry who could speak to her skill set and unique talents. While she was not surprised to learn she was underpaid, she was shocked to discover that many of her comparable peers were earning almost double her salary and receiving a more robust benefits package.

Anna calmly and intelligently shared her research with David, backing it up with hard numbers and pointing to specific times when her involvement increased revenue for both David and his clients. She then stated her new requested salary, which was on par with industry standards. In lieu of the rich benefits package that many of her peers received, she requested a flexible work schedule on Tuesdays as well as Friday afternoons, which would allow her to have the adaptability often needed when caring for a baby during its first year of life.

David's jaw practically fell on the floor. "So, you're telling me you want *that* salary for *part-time* work?"

Anna assured David, "I'm still willing to travel on weekends and be available after work hours for client emergencies or planned events. And as usual, I would not be requesting additional compensation for that time." She went on to remind David, "I know how we have discussed at length how time is relatively irrelevant in our positions. And I want to reiterate that I would still be available on those days if needed. Having a flexible work schedule a day and a half out of the week would be a huge benefit to me in this new stage of life."

"I'll need some time to consider it, Anna. I need to consult with my accountant and reconsider how this new schedule would affect operations," David explained matter-of-factly. While David's tone was kind, Anna had worked for him long enough to know he was not pleased with her request.

Three days later, David called Anna with an update. "Anna, I understand where your salary request is coming from," he began, "and there is no doubt that you have been a valuable member of my company for the past three years. But the fact is, I'm just not comfortable paying that kind of salary and would rather use those resources in other areas of the business."

Anna felt the room slightly tilt on its axis. While she was expecting that David would not want to pay the requested salary, she was anticipating a negotiation or potentially even some sort of bonus structure to be offered—something, *or really anything*, that was a monetary reflection of the value that he said she brought to the company. Anna took a deep breath. "I understand where you are coming from, David. But the truth of the matter is that I simply cannot afford to continue working for you at my current salary. With the skyrocketing cost of living in our city and the growth of my family, it financially does not make any sense for me to continue working at this rate. I would *lose* money working for you under our old setup." Anna disclosed this information, hopeful that it would open David's eyes to what it would mean to continue at her current salary and inspire at least some negotiation.

"I understand," David went on in a kind voice. "If you're unable to continue working for me at this current salary, I think we should part ways. I am more than happy to provide any work references as you look for a position that would be better suited for your needs."

David had just made three of the biggest mistakes you can make as a CEO whose company has experienced rapid growth:

1. He underappreciated his employee's contribution to the company during a time of high growth.

2. He did not compensate his employee according to her performance.

3. He refused to consider Anna's changes in personal and professional goals and work to retain her.

Unless you come into a giant windfall of cash, or even if you do, parting with a large sum of money is never "comfortable" for any CEO. As you have probably guessed, faced with the ultimatum, Anna had no option but to leave the company, the position, and the CEO that she, just days before, was excited to continue working for. David's shortsightedness may have kept his financials comfortable that quarter, but he paid dearly in the long run.

The fallout of Anna's departure was felt almost immediately. When David shared the news with the remaining team, they were absolutely devastated. Yes, they had all been managing while Anna was on maternity leave, but now they were overwhelmed by the sheer volume of work that would need to be absorbed by a team that David was no longer willing to grow. Additionally, with the loss of institutional knowledge and direction that Anna provided regularly, the team was often confused regarding vision and context. As you can imagine, the efficiency and quality of work of each team member were affected for at least six months while they attempted to fill the void in Anna's absence.

David was not immune to the wakes caused by Anna's departure. Most pressingly, his time was mostly absorbed back into managing the day-to-day operations of his company and employees. The time he would have spent proactively strategizing his client's careers with label reps and touring agents, he was now using to put out fires for his employees. Next, he keenly felt Anna's loss in her strategic and intuitive approach to both his needs and their clients. Anna had a knack for sensing when a client, or their family, would be in need of a break from the demands of being a recording and touring artist and would often suggest they bake in time off during their strategic planning meetings for the upcoming year.

Yet, the loss that stung the most was that of a trusted friend and of someone who, for all intents and purposes, served as a business partner to David. As their career manager, David was the person his clients turned to when they felt discouraged, tired, or confused about the next right step. David realized that Anna had often served as that to him. Now, he mostly felt increasingly isolated.

Anna, on the other hand, was just fine; she was almost immediately offered a position at a rival company that offered her almost double the salary that she had requested from David. This was a company that understood talent when it saw it and was more than willing to make the investment.

Many companies, like David's, after a season of growth, then experience an exodus of employees. While some employees may have been offered higher compensation, or some may have had a change in their personal life, it all comes down to the same conclusion:

The employee has deemed the opportunity you offer not a worthwhile investment of their time, energy, or talent.

Many CEOs still believe we are stuck back in the days when someone should consider themselves lucky to have a job, when the truth is if you're lucky enough to find a great employee, you should bend over backward to incentivize them to stay. Times of high growth often serve as a refining process for both CEOs and their teams. Like gold heated to a high temperature, the pressure from times of immense growth makes it very easy to see who's made of gold, their talents become evident, and they succeed more easily than others. A similar process can be said of CEOs; how a CEO treats their employees after these seasons informs employees if they have a long-term future in the company.

> **If you're lucky enough to find a great employee, you should bend over backward to incentivize them to stay.**

Retaining those gold employees is critical not only in surviving growth, which is often stressful and strenuous, but also for long-term success. These are the employees you want with you ten, fifteen, or even twenty years from now. They will be the ones you want to carry on your legacy after you're gone.

To do this, you'll have to be proactive in not making the same critical mistakes our friend David did.

1. Be sure to appreciate your employees' contributions, especially in a time of high growth.

Like Anna, many employees, from your direct reports to your entry-level positions, are bringing their best to their role day in and day out, hoping the investment in your company will result in long-term opportunities for their professional growth. Yes, David had invested in Anna, but Anna had also invested in the company. And that is what many CEOs fail to recognize when it comes to showing appreciation to their employees. Their standard paycheck or the year-end Christmas party is not adequate compensation for an employee who goes above and beyond. And while offering her the COO promotion was a nice gesture, it was ultimately a shallow one, as he was only offering her more work and responsibility without any benefits. Just as you wouldn't retain an employee whose standard of work was on the floor, employees no longer commit to remaining with employers whose standards of appreciation are in the basement.

2. Compensate employees according to their performance.

Going hand in hand with appreciation, if you want to retain those gold-standard employees, you must consistently offer them gold-standard compensation. If you do not, someone else will. Jumping to another company doesn't mean they aren't loyal to you. Just as you are the CEO of your company, each employee is the CEO of their career, and you have to make the numbers make sense.

Employees like Anna are willing to play the long game and invest their time and talents in your company. So when you invest financially in your employees, it always pays off in the long run.

3. Consider changes in their personal and professional goals, and work to accommodate them as best you can.

If you're lucky, an employee will remain with you from three to five years, and hopefully longer. A lot can happen in someone's life in that span of time. An employee who is a recent college graduate can easily get married and start a family. God forbid, but often people receive life-changing diagnoses for themselves or a family member. Kids turn into teens who start driving, renters become homeowners, and so on. While it may not be possible to know the intimate details of each of your employees' personal lives, you should have a pulse on what is happening in the company and do your best to stay ahead of the curve.

From offering legal insurance, remote working options, paid parental leave, or a better medical package, these benefits can signifi-cantly affect the personal lives of your employees. They can be the difference between someone staying with you and being hired out from under you.

When it comes down to it, those gold-standard employees will always be a financial investment, but good people are the best financial investment you can make. When needing to make a hard choice, always choose to invest in your people. When you do so, success is inevitable, and the growth you're hoping for will always come in its wake.

> When needing to make a hard choice, always choose to invest in your people.

EDIT YOUR PRACTICES AND SYSTEMS

Twenty years ago, Ross, who we met back in chapter 1, started out working in the warehouse of his father's company. His dad figured it was a grunt job that Ross would quit before the end of the summer and never ask his dad for a job again. Fast-forward, and not only did Ross dominate in his warehouse job, but over the next fifteen years, he slowly but surely worked his way up in the company. Five years ago, Ross took on the role of CEO from his father, and in just a couple of years he grew the company grossing $20 million a year to $100 million a year.

The great part about Ross having worked every job in the company is that he knew the ins and outs of how every department should run. Unfortunately, for some CEOs this familiarity can also serve as a stumbling block.

When Ross was preparing for his one-month sabbatical, he did a fantastic job empowering his leadership team to run things in his absence. Upon his return, Ross was pleased to find that things were humming along nicely. Client accounts were in order, sales were looking great, and nothing catastrophic had happened.

Then Ross walked into the warehouse, only to discover they had overhauled their systems. Immediately he could spot a couple of dozen things he would do differently. The warehouse was his baby, it was where he had cut his professional teeth, and obviously the department means a lot to him personally. Ross's COO found him back in the warehouse two hours later, reorganizing the entire operation. For Ross is an incredible strategist, a hard-working CEO, and his employees are very loyal. So in the grand scheme of things he had a good laugh with the warehouse team and everyone went about their day.

But unlike Ross, the CEOs who I see repeatedly get stuck are the ones that refuse to allow systems to grow and evolve along with the company. This could be a recurring meeting that isn't actually helpful toward productivity, or perhaps a system of reporting and data tracking that no longer suits your needs. A lot of times it becomes easy to mark something new as incorrect.

I am not immune to this either. When I am coaching my clients, my "warehouse" is the specific solutions and processes that worked for me when I was in the C-suite office. But each of my clients has a different business, industry, company culture, and education. What worked for me may not work for them. That is why I always hold back on giving a specific process or solution. Instead I lead with questions, and, without criticizing, we follow them one by one until we reveal the answer.

We all have our own "warehouses," or areas of business where we are comfortable, and where it's difficult to imagine it operating differently. But just like a captain cannot lead a ship if they are constantly in the boiler room, a CEO cannot run a company from the warehouse. It's incredibly important that we don't interfere unless we are being asked to speak into a solution.

To cut loose the practices or systems that are no longer serving your company, there are a few things you will need to keep in mind.

1. If you're micromanaging, you're not acting as the CEO, and the person you hired is not doing their job.

The best thing you can do for your company is to hire someone you trust and get out of their way. Accept that they will do things differently than you, and being different is not wrong. As long as they deliver on their goals and KPIs, let their process be their process.

2. Delegate as quickly as possible.

As the CEO, it's often tempting, especially during times of transition, to take on a role or responsibility that you're familiar with, with the intention of passing it off or hiring someone in six months, when the truth is, the longer you hold onto it, the more difficult it will become to pass it off. Delegate anything not in line with your job as a CEO as quickly as possible.

3. Take a thirty-day sabbatical at least once a year.

As I've mentioned in previous chapters, you should be able to walk away from your business at any point and trust that your leadership team can manage in the short run. A great practice to establish is to once a year take a thirty-day sabbatical. It will keep you in the habit of setting up systems and processes that are not dependent upon you for day-to-day operations.

CONSIDER YOUR EXIT PLAN

In the midst of writing this book, the esteemed journalist Barbara Walters passed away at ninety-three years old. Everywhere you looked, there was another moving tribute to her esteemed career. She was the first woman to co-anchor a network evening news broadcast and interviewed every sitting president from Nixon to Obama. While she has developed a signature interview style that is studied in journalism classes and won dozens of awards for her outstanding reporting, she considers none of these accomplishments as her legacy.

When asked, Barbara always described that she was most proud of the fact that she trailblazed a path for other women in journalism. When sharing her intentions for retiring, she explained, "I want instead to sit in a sunny field and admire the very gifted women—OK, some men too—who will be taking my place."[19]

From the beginning, Barbara had the end of her career in mind and understood that her legacy was not the awards or the accolades but the people she could impact and empower. She was committed to something that we as CEOs often forget: you have to build with your exit plan in mind. At each stage of growth, you should anticipate your exit and how to do it well.

When Barbara made her last appearance on the hit daytime television show she founded, *The View*, Oprah Winfrey joined the table that morning to pay tribute to Walters. "I had to be here for your last show, to celebrate you, because of what you have meant to me," Winfrey told Walters. "You have literally meant the world to me. ... Like everyone else, I want to thank you for being a pioneer and everything that word means. It means being the first; the first in the

---

19   "Barbara Walters, Groundbreaking TV Journalist, Dies at 93," CBS News, December 31, 2022, https://www.cbsnews.com/news/barbara-walters-dies-age-93-groundbreaking-tv-journalist/.

room to knock down the door, to break down the barriers, to pave the road that we all walk on. I thank you for that. And I thank you for the courage it took every day to get up and keep doing it" (Sullivan).[20] The stage was then flooded by twenty-five of the most prestigious women in American journalism, from Katie Couric to Gayle King, Jane Paulie, and more.

Creating a successful exit plan and leaving a legacy that will withstand the test of time have little to do with record profits and everything to do with the people you impact.

You should constantly consider and evaluate your leadership team and the effect your decisions have on them. Is there a place for them in your organization long term? Are you carving a path that like-minded people would be proud to follow?

> Creating a successful exit plan and leaving a legacy that will withstand the test of time have little to do with record profits and everything to do with the people you impact.

If not, this needs to be priority number one. Because while your company may survive the next phase of growth, your legacy will only survive as long as the positive impact you create for other people.

---

20 Marisa Sullivan, "Barbara Walters' Final Episode of *The View* Included an Epic Surprise," *People*, December 31, 2022, https://people.com/tv/how-barbara-walters-said-goodbye-to-the-view/.

Questions from the Vault

1. Think of at least one "Anna" in your company. What can you do to reward and compensate this golden employee according to their value and their needs?

2. What is one practice that needs to be cut loose or reevaluated? Not sure? Ask your COO. They probably have a list.

3. Have you created or updated your exit plan recently? If not, create or review one in the next thirty days, review it with your COO and your partner to get their thoughts, and discuss what needs to change today so that you are on track.

CHAPTER TWELVE
People First

---

*"GREAT LEADERS TRULY CARE ABOUT THOSE
THEY ARE PRIVILEGED TO LEAD AND UNDER-
STAND THAT THE TRUE COST OF THE LEADER-
SHIP PRIVILEGE COMES AT THE EXPENSE OF
SELF-INTEREST."*

—SIMON SINEK, LEADERS EAT LAST: WHY SOME
TEAMS PULL TOGETHER AND OTHERS DON'T

Just about anyone in business is familiar with former Starbucks CEO Howard Schultz's famous quote, "We're not in the coffee business. It's what we sell as a product, but we're in the people business."[21] It's one of those quotes you hear tossed around by branding professionals or speakers weave into their content at leadership conferences. It sounds great, and we're usually willing to acknowledge the wisdom

---

21 Carmine Gallo, "Starbucks CEO: Lesson in Communication Skills," YouTube, https://www.forbes.com/sites/carminegallo/2011/03/25/starbucks-ceo-lesson-in-communication-skills/?sh=280d596d72b8.

behind it, but many of us pay it as much heed as we do our New Year's resolutions on February 1st: a goal we want to keep in mind, but something you have to balance amid the real demands of the business. But this concept is more than a tired trope; it's the cornerstone of every good business practice and the critical differentiator between having a simply profitable business and a truly great one.

Schultz has a long and established history with the coffee colossus Starbucks. Starting with the company in 1982, he served as CEO from 1986 to 2000. In those fourteen years, he was instrumental in growing the company from a local Seattle coffee shop to a brand name synonymous with coffee. People don't just grab a cup of coffee anymore; they go for "a Starbucks." In 2000, he stepped down as CEO but remained part of the board while continuing to pursue other endeavors. Then in 2008, the great recession hit, and despite Starbucks's brand strength and years of sales, like every other business at the time, the company began to struggle. At this point, Schultz was asked to return as CEO and, hopefully, save the ship from sinking.

In an interview with *Harvard Business Review*, Schultz shares his experience as he faced one tough decision after another in a bid to save the company. Surprise, surprise, he made a lot of stakeholders nervous with decisions that reinforced and doubled down on company values and culture. When responding to their skepticism, he did so with humility, unblinking responsibility, and dedicated belief that the values they founded the company on would see them through these obstacles. "You can't get out of this by trying to navigate with a different road map, one that isn't true to yourself. You have to be authentic, you have to be true, and you have to believe in your heart that this is going to work."[22]

---

22 Adi Ignatius, "The HBR Interview: "We Had to Own the Mistakes,"" *Harvard Business Review*, https://hbr.org/2010/07/the-hbr-interview-we-had-to-own-the-mistakes.

At significant cost to the company, he organized a mandatory three-hour retraining for all employees, then flew over ten thousand managers to New Orleans to impress upon them the direness of the situation and the commitment that would be required by each of them. It was critical that every customer interaction was superb. Schultz explained, "Quintessentially, we are a people-based company. You couldn't find another consumer brand that is as dependent on human behavior as we are. We built Starbucks not through traditional marketing or advertising but through the experience. And that experience can come to life only if people are proud, if they respect and trust the green apron and the people they are representing."[23]

> Plain and simple, every successful company is a people company.

Repeatedly, Howard Schultz very clearly defines the one thing that truly sets apart successful companies from companies that are merely profitable. Plain and simple, every successful company is a people company. Sure, they sell a product or offer a service, but the lifeblood of their business is the people who work for them, and they never forget it, even when it's inconvenient or painful.

GENUINELY CARE AND SHOW IT

Unfortunately, many CEOs conduct business as if giving someone a paycheck exempts us from treating them like living, breathing human beings. Rather, we approach our employees as just another resource we have to manage. We say things like "It's not personal; it's business" as an excuse to say or do things that are detrimental to the mental, emotional, and physical health of our employees. If no one has said

---

23   Ibid.

this to you before, I am happy to be the first; your title, your profit margin, or your bonus structure does not give you the license to be a horrible person.

So many of the issues CEOs face in their companies today could be completely eliminated if they would simply genuinely care about their people and show it. Yes, some of the ways you show you care will require a financial investment, like adequate paid time off and offering a competitive benefits package. But guess what happens when your employees don't burn out and are in good health? They do amazing work; they contribute creative solutions that result in increased profits; they don't quit or search for higher-paying jobs. There are also many ways to show you care and appreciate your employees that are completely free.

With my coaching clients, we meet as a group once a month and rotate who hosts the group and provides lunch that day. Recently we were hosted by Nate, my coaching client, who has taken to heart what it means to care about his employees and doesn't hesitate to show it.

As everyone in our group made their lunch plates and began to eat, we were amazed by the delicious food. Many of the dishes we had never seen or tasted before. The combination of flavors and the level they were prepared was nothing short of sheer perfection. Every one of our groups went back for seconds or dessert because we could not help ourselves.

As we finished lunch, Nate ushered into the conference room a middle-aged man of Middle Eastern descent. "Hey everyone!" he called our attention to the front. "This is George," he began affectionately, placing a hand on the man's shoulders, "he is the one who made lunch, and he is by far the best caterer I have ever worked with. Next time you need someone, he is the man and will give you the hookup." As Nate introduced George, you could see a look of shyness cross his face as he was showered with honor in front of a dozen millionaires. The room stood and applauded the chef for his amazing artistry.

Showing honor and appreciation to George at that moment was not something Nate needed to do. It's not in George's contract or work arrangement that Nate delivers a special thanks or provides a certain number of referrals. Nate genuinely cares about George's success, and it cost him practically nothing, barely even thirty seconds of his time, to show his appreciation. Needless to say, George will be incredibly loyal to Nate for the rest of his professional career.

SERVE THOSE YOU LEAD

Throughout this book, we've continually used the analogy between a CEO and a ship's captain, defining the role as charting the destination, empowering each employee to their job with little to no interference from you, and making overarching decisions that benefit the long-term health of the company. But there is an undercurrent to this role that is important to understand if you want to be a great captain: You are, first and foremost, a servant to those you lead.

To clarify, servant leadership does not mean you take on tasks that you've hired someone else to do. Rather, it sets the tone for how you lead, how you speak to your employees, and the culture of the company.

When I was running that Harley shop in St. Augustine, Florida, I had an amazing tech; we'll call him Ben. He was fantastic with clients, a killer department manager, and one of the most knowledgeable technicians I had ever worked with. I had been working with him for over a year and never once had one single issue. So I was shocked to come in one day to find a very upset customer complaining that Ben had been rude to them, and they were very dissatisfied with their service.

Unfortunately, I did not have my servant leadership hat on that day. I promptly grabbed the store manager, found Ben, and reamed him out in front of the entire team of techs in the service garage. I felt the need to flex my authority and let him know that his behavior was unacceptable. I viewed my role as owner and CEO as an excuse to be rude, critical, and angry; I saw my role that day as someone who needed to bring down the hammer rather than someone who is there to serve. It should come as no surprise when I tell you that two weeks later, Ben put in his notice. He was going to work for one of my competitors. I immediately knew that it was my actions that day that caused him to resign; I deeply apologized and asked if there was anything I could do to make him stay. He politely declined, which I completely understood, and that day I lost one of the best employees I have ever worked with.

In hindsight, I see how things would have been completely different if I had approached the situation as a servant leader. I would have led with questions, asking for Ben's side of the story first. Also, remember that this has *never* happened before and outside of his character. My next step should have been to ask him if anything was going on that caused him to feel stressed that day and treat the customer in that manner. Maybe he was short-staffed, or maybe the new software we had switched over to was acting up and making his life miserable. A servant leader would have seen Ben first and foremost as a human being, and just like me, he would have good days and bad.

The tone I struck that day in the garage was, "This *will* never happen again!" If I had taken the approach of a servant leader, my tone would have been, "How can I help so that this never happens again?"

Either way, I needed to have a hard conversation with Ben, just like you will have hard conversations with employees in the future. The tone with which you have the conversations is everything.

CREATE A GREAT EMPLOYEE EXPERIENCE

Good leaders know their people and understand what they need to have a great employee experience. This begins first and foremost by learning to lead with kindness, compassion, gentleness, curiosity, love, and humor. The alpha bravado we often see in leaders is off-putting, passing themselves off as some sort of modern-day Greek god that parades themselves high above everyone else. Projecting yourself as a Greek god doesn't inspire confidence in your teams. It breeds resentment.

Yes, lead with confidence, but your confidence should be born of your care for your employees and your belief in their abilities to do an excellent job, not in your ego. Employees don't need to see you as above it all; they need to see you as a human. You set the atmosphere for the office, and you also set the tone for how your employees treat your clients and customers.

Creating a great employee experience is more than ping-pong tables in the break room and keeping the fridge stocked with snacks. It's creating a culture where questions are welcomed and innovative ideas are encouraged. A great employee experience is one where they are often praised for contributions, both outstanding and mundane, and their excellence isn't rewarded with more work. So many times, it's the employees who show up well every day and quietly do great work that are passed over and forgotten. Their plates are stacked full with more work because they are reliable and trustworthy. How would their experience change if your posture toward them was "What can I do for you?" rather than "Get it done!"?

Throughout this book, I've shared multiple examples of CEOs who repeatedly have issues stemming from how they value people. For the past eleven chapters, I have given you very specific tools, and each of them comes back to these three main strategies:

- Care about your people and show it.

- Serve those you lead.

- Create a great employee experience.

In the same interview with *Harvard Business Review,* Howard Shultz shared something incredibly profound that drives this point home: "We live amid a fracturing of civility. Everywhere we go as consumers, we're getting people who don't want to reach into our hearts or know who we are; they want to reach into our wallets and get some money. The equity of the brand is defined by the quality of the coffee but also, most importantly, by the relationship that the barista has with the customer and whether or not the customer feels valued, appreciated, and respected. That is our aspiration every day."

The quality of the relationship your team has with your customers and clients begins with *you.* Creating a space where employees feel valued, appreciated, and respected should be your daily aspiration. When in doubt—whether you're feeling stuck or it looks like the end is coming—the people who work for you come first. Sometimes that may even mean firing a client or a high-performing team member who is cruel to others. These are the defining moments where you will need to choose between being an amazing people company and being a standard company that simply makes a profit.

As Schultz was attempting to right the ship after the crash of the economy in 2008, one of the biggest ways he decided to remain a people company was the moment he refused to cut employee medical benefits. The company's healthcare costs for the previous year were approximately $300 million as Starbucks offers these benefits to any eligible employee who works at least twenty hours a week. "The thought that we would cut that benefit—I couldn't do it. Within this past year I got a call from one of our institutional shareholders. He said, 'You've never had more cover to cut healthcare than you do now. No one will criticize you.' And I just said, 'I could cut $300 million out of a lot of things, but do you want to kill the company, and kill the trust in what this company stands for? There is no way I will do it, and if that is what you want us to do, you should sell your stock.' What I stand for is not just to make money; it's to preserve the integrity of what we have built for thirty-nine years—to look in the mirror and feel like I've done something that has meaning and relevancy and is something people are going to respect. You have to be willing to fight for what you believe in."

> The fastest way to sabotage your company is to not care about the employee experience. Subsequently, the best way to grow a thriving, healthy, sustainable business that can stand the test of time is to prioritize your employee experience.

The fastest way to sabotage your company is to not care about the employee experience. Subsequently, the best way to grow a thriving, healthy, sustainable business that can stand the test of time is to prioritize your employee experience. Either way the way you treat your employees, your mentors, your leadership team, and the people in your life will define your legacy.

You get to choose what people say about you after you're gone, not through a will or some document, but in your daily interactions with the people you see every day. Choose to put your people first, and choose to be a people company. When you do you grow strong, and stronger roots will ensure your company and legacy can withstand any storm.

Questions from the Vault

1. Connect with your mentors and ask for their honest feedback on your leadership tone. Do you take the tone of a Greek god who wants to be feared or that of a servant leader who desires to help?

2. Where has the employee experience been lacking in my company or not kept up with competitors?

www.ingramcontent.com/pod-product-compliance
Lightning Source LLC
Chambersburg PA
CBHW020455100426
42813CB00031B/3372/J